*This book is dedicated to the memory of
Jeffrey Christopher Cwikiel (1971-1996)
in honor of his love for Michigan's lakes,
rivers, streams, and wetlands.*

Living With Michigan's Wetlands
A Landowner's Guide

Author
Wilfred Cwikiel

Illustrator
Thomas W. Ford

Can you Identify the Following Species on the Front Cover?

Great Blue Heron	Northern Water Snake	Pickerel Weed
Northern Harrier	Eastern Painted Turtle	Blue-flag Iris
Marsh Wren	Leopard Frog	Arrowhead
Wood Duck	Short-stalked Damsel Fly	Cattail
Trumpeter Swan	Twelve-spot Skimmer	Wild Rice
Red-winged Blackbird	River Otter	Pond Lily
American Bittern	White-tailed Deer	
Four-toed Salamander	Muskrat	

The purpose of this document is to promote wetland stewardship by private landowners. If you would like to reproduce this book or portions of it for reasons consistent with this purpose, please contact the publisher:

Tip of the Mitt Watershed Council
P.O. Box 300
Conway, MI 49722
PH: (616) 347-1181
FX: (616) 347-5928

This book shall be cited as follows:
Cwikiel, Wilfred. *Living With Michigan's Wetlands: A Landowner's Guide*
Tip of the Mitt Watershed Council, Conway, MI 1996

Funding for this project was made possible by a grant from the U.S. Environmental Protection Agency to the Michigan Department of Environmental Quality (Federal Grant # CD995523-01-0).

Table of Contents

Acknowledgments

The most important acknowledgment for the book goes to Michigan's wetlands. These areas of biological productivity and scenic beauty served as the inspiration for this publication.

This book was made possible by the financial support of the U.S. Environmental Protection Agency through their Wetland Protection State Development Grant Program. In addition to this guidebook, this grant program has provided Michigan and many other states with grant dollars to help fund the efforts of state agencies to effectively protect, manage, and restore wetland resources.

Thomas W. Ford and Katherine Melby contributed greatly to the final beauty and form of the book. I would like to thank the staff of the Tip of the Mitt Watershed Council for their support and assistance throughout the project. Ann Baughman, Doug Fuller, and Scott McEwen proved indispensable in reviewing drafts of the text and easing my workload so I could focus on this project. I'd especially like to thank Jan Wilkins, Administrative Assistant, for her willingness to lend a hand on any task, and Gail Gruenwald, Executive Director, for her vision and leadership. I would especially like to acknowledge Debbie Messer's willingness to take on the painstaking task of reviewing the text for typographic errors. I would also like to acknowledge the National Wetlands Conservation Alliance for developing a model Wetlands Assistance Guide which proved to be helpful.

This publication would not have been possible without the efforts of many individuals, foremost among them the private landowners and professionals who performed the valuable function of reviewing the text. The review panel was comprised of individuals and groups that represent the interests of property owners in the context of wetland conservation and protection. It is important to note that by serving as reviewers, the individuals listed below do not necessarily endorse every opinion expressed in this document and their listing here does not imply responsibility for the text. They did, however, play a valuable role in this project and/or the establishment of Michigan's Wetland Conservation Strategy, and deserve individual acknowledgment here.

Thomas Bailey
Little Traverse Conservancy

Chuck Becker
Publishing Paper Division/
Woodland Department
Mead Paper Company

Peg Bostwick
Land and Water Management Division
Michigan Department of Environmental
Quality

Mike Boyce
Michigan Audubon Society

Michael Finnigan and Sheryl Brown
Private Landowners

Carolyn Bury
Region V, U.S. Environmental
Protection Agency

Glen Chown
Grand Traverse Regional
Land Conservancy

Carla Clos
Meridian Township Environmental
Commission

Rod Cortright
MSU Extension

Dave Dempsey
Michigan Environmental Council

Walter Gauthier
U.S. Army Corps of Engineers

Jim Goodheart
Pheasants Forever, Inc.

Gail Gruenwald
Tip of the Mitt Watershed Council

Woody Held
Johnson, Johnson, & Roy, Inc.

Fred Hingst
Ducks Unlimited, Inc.

Jim Hudgins
U.S. Fish and Wildlife Service

Kevin Kirk
Michigan Farm Bureau

Gerald Martz
Wildlife Division
Michigan Department of Natural
Resources

Ed McCarthy
Wildlife Unlimited-Delta County

Dr. James and Sue McGillicuddy
Private Landowners

Debbie Messer
Private Landowner

Richard X. Moore
Michigan United Conservation Clubs

Allan S. Puplis
Wetland Conservation Association

Donald Reinke
U.S. Army Corps of Engineers

Paul Rentschler
Huron River Watershed Council

Lynn Sampson
U.S. Department of Agriculture
Natural Resources Conservation Service

Lori Sargent
Wildlife Division
Michigan Department of Natural
Resources

Steven Shine
Michigan Department of Agriculture
Farmland Services

Marilyn Shy
Michigan Association of Conservation
Districts

Bob Sweet
Surface Water Quality Division
Michigan Department of Environmental
Quality

Maureen Kennedy Templeton
Grand Traverse County
Drain Commissioner

Pam Tyning, Director
Michigan Chapter, North American
Lake Management Society

Jack Walker
Michigan Association of Realtors

Lisa Warner
Land and Water Management Division
Michigan Department of Environmental
Quality

William Weiss
Elk-Skegemog Lakes Association
Three Lakes Association
Red Mule Engineering

Rick Wilson
Leelanau Conservancy

Don Winne
Michigan Lakes and Streams Assn.

Helen Willis
Michigan Society of Planning Officials

Tom Woiwode
The Nature Conservancy

Preface

This book is based on the belief that Michigan's wetland property owners care about their property and want to manage it in the best way possible. Private landowners value land in many different ways. In addition to using their land as a place to live or work, many landowners enjoy the natural and cultural resource values of their property for recreation or to otherwise enhance the quality of their lives. Many landowners have long practiced voluntary land and water conservation as a way to manage and retain the special natural and cultural values of their property. This type of individual stewardship has contributed considerably to meeting state and national conservation goals.

Private landowners also value their land as an economic investment and a source of income. The economic value or potential of a property is of great importance to the owner and influences decisions made about existing and future use of the land. As a result, the conservation of wetlands and riparian habitats on private lands requires an approach which is sensitive to: 1) the economic value of land, 2) the landowner's long- and short-range plans for and expectations of the property, and 3) the landowner's present economic situation.

The purpose of this document is to help landowners understand wetlands, the benefits of wetlands, basic techniques and options for wetland management, the economic benefits of various protection methods, and where to go for more assistance. The information in this book is meant to help you make decisions regarding protection of wetlands and other natural resources while meeting your economic needs and personal goals. All efforts were made to insure that the information contained in this document regarding current regulations and government programs was up to date at the time of publication. However, given the potential for changes in funding for incentive programs and legislation for regulatory programs, you should make sure programs are intact before integrating them into your wetland management plans.

The purpose of this book is to serve as your information resource. It is designed in a way that does not require reading each chapter in order. Feel free to skip around and read those chapters that interest you most. Chapter 1 presents and promotes the concept of wetland owners as important stewards. Chapters 2-4 provide basic information on wetlands and how you can learn more about your particular wetland. Chapter 5 provides a strategy to help landowners choose the best conservation and management options for their particular situation. Chapter 6 explains some of the voluntary mechanisms used to protect wetlands, many of which bring financial benefits to landowners. Chapters 7-8 provide background on activities that impact wetlands and ways to manage wetlands to protect and enhance their functional values. Chapter 9 provides information on current wetland regulations that every landowner should know. Chapter 10 provides information on where to go for more help. The appendices serve as your resource list for agencies and nonprofit organizations working to assist landowners in conserving their wetlands.

March 14, 1996

Dear Landowner:

I am pleased to welcome you to "<u>Living with Michigan's Wetlands: A Landowners Guide</u>". Wetlands are an essential element of Michigan's landscape and environment. These extraordinary tracts of land provide a home and habitat for Michigan's abundant wildlife and are also an integral component of our delicate ecosystem.

Society's understanding of the many functions and values that wetlands provide continues to grow. In addition to important fish and wildlife habitat, wetlands protect us from floods, maintain water quality, protect vulnerable aquifers, and provide aesthetic values. Because the functions that wetlands provide are valuable to society, wetland protection benefits the public. In Michigan, where a large part of our economy is based on clean water and abundant fish and wildlife, wetland protection is especially important.

Government regulation of wetlands can offer only a part of the solution. Ultimately, the individual wetland property owners will be the stewards that ensure wetland protection in this state.

This book is here for you, the wetland property owner, to help you manage your wetland for your personal benefit, and the benefit of all. By wisely managing your wetland to maintain or enhance its natural functions, you are providing an example to the rest of us to be considerate of our neighbors and leave the world a better place for the next generation.

Sincerely,

John Engler
Governor

Wetlands and You:
A Call to Stewardship

The word "wetlands" conjures up many images: a flight of ducks at sunset, a dark and mysterious swamp, delicate orchids blooming, and of course, a regal Great Blue Heron standing like a statue. In addition to their beauty, wetlands are some of our most valuable ecological resources. Wetlands provide us with important functions that enhance our quality of life. As a private landowner, you have an important role to play in wetland protection and management.

The Michigan Department of Environmental Quality estimates that over 75% of Michigan's wetlands are privately owned. Probably an even greater percentage of the potentially restorable wetlands occur on private property. Private land owners are ultimately responsible for the level of protection that a particular wetland receives and whether or not a former wetland will be restored.

In 1949, Aldo Leopold's *A Sand County Almanac* was published. That book presents the concept of land stewardship. Professor Leopold, a wildlife biologist, encouraged us to realize that all things are connected and to think about the long-term implications of our land management activities. In essence, he urges us to consider the implications of our actions on the entire ecological system, and then act in a way that maintains its integrity. By maintaining ecological integrity, he contends, we would guarantee a functioning ecosystem that ultimately benefits all plant, animal, and human members.

Nowhere are the benefits of environmental stewardship more evident than with wetlands. Property owners benefit from wetland protection in many ways. Most obviously, they have their own nature preserve that provides opportunities for a range of recreational activities. Even very small wetlands can provide an excellent stage upon which to view the drama of nature. If you are fortunate enough to have wetlands that border a lake or stream, you directly benefit from the water quality and erosion control functions of wetlands. For some landowners, the privacy that wetlands offer by serving as a natural sound and visual buffer between other

homes, commercial uses, and roads is its most valuable function.

Wetland benefits go beyond property boundaries. Many birds use wetlands at every stop in their migration from their summer homes in the arctic to their winter

homes in the tropics. Wetlands help protect property owners from flooding, maintain the quality of our lakes and rivers, and provide fish and wildlife habitat. Wetlands that protect vulnerable aquifers benefit everyone who draws drinking water from them. Wetlands provide habitat for endangered plants and animals—an important part of our natural heritage. Because the functions of wetlands benefit people other than the property owner (and conversely, wetland losses impact people other than the property owner), wetland landowners have a higher call to be good stewards than most landowners. In addition to maintaining ecosystem integrity, good wetland stewards are good neighbors who accept their responsibility to manage their land in a way that does not harm others.

Unfortunately, Michigan and the United States have lost alarming amounts of wetlands. Since European settlement, the lower 48 United States have lost over 53% of their original wetlands. In the most recent survey conducted by the U.S. Fish and Wildlife Service, Michigan has lost 50% of its original wetlands. The percentage of Michigan's coastal wetlands that have been lost is even greater—70%. In total, over 5,600,000 acres of wetlands have been destroyed in Michigan.

It is hard to quantify all that we have lost with the conversion of so many millions of acres of wetlands. We can get an idea of the substantial losses by considering the increases in flood damage, the degraded water quality, the number of wetland species that have become extinct, the reduced populations of waterfowl, and many other indicators of poor ecosystem health. Another way to visualize the impacts of wetland conversion in Michigan is to consider that we now only have one-half of the valuable functions that wetlands provide.

When we consider that over 50% of Michigan's wetlands are gone and that 75% of Michigan's remaining wetlands are in private ownership, we can see how crucial it is that wetland property owners answer the call to stewardship.

As you will see in the following chapters, there are many ways to become a wetland steward. Wetland stewardship does not obligate you to costly or time-consuming activities. In fact, what you don't do is often more important to good stewardship than what you do. For example, a "hands-off" approach may be the best option for a well-functioning, intact wetland.

Wetland stewardship can be very rewarding. If you are like most Americans, you support protecting our country's rich natural heritage. Being a good wetland steward is one of the most beneficial ways to contribute to a quality environment for this and future generations. In addition to the benefits that you will receive, you will have the satisfaction of knowing that you helped to ensure good water quality, flood protection, and abundant fish and wildlife for your neighbors.

Aldo Leopold wrote that, "the evolution of a land ethic is an intellectual as well as emotional process." Many wetland owners care deeply for their land. As you learn more about your wetland through this book and your own stewardship activities, the emotional bond between you, your family, and the land will surely increase. As this happens, Michigan's wetland property owners will take the lead in developing a more positive relationship between the people and the land.

Wetlands: A Valuable Resource

What are wetlands? Why are wetlands important? When this country was first settled by Europeans, not all the functions of wetlands were recognized, let alone valued as important to society. Through the work of scientists, hunters, anglers, naturalists, and land managers, we are now better able to answer these questions than ever before.

WHAT ARE WETLANDS?

Wetlands are unique and varied ecosystems that are too wet to be considered upland, and too dry to be considered "deep water" habitats. In other words, to borrow an old farm adage, wetlands are "too thick to drink and too thin to plow." Michigan is fortunate to contain a diversity of wetland types ranging from broad expanses of coastal marsh to small isolated bogs. Numerous terms have developed over the years to describe different types of wetlands across the United States.

Michigan's wetland regulatory statute clumps the many different wetland types into three categories: marsh, swamp, and bog (northern peatland). Below are general descriptions of the wetlands that occur in these categories. For a discussion on wetland determination and delineation, see Chapter 3.

Marsh

When people hear the term wetland, they most commonly think of a marsh. Marsh is a term that represents a broad array of wetlands that are dominated by grasslike vegetation. Typical marsh plants include rushes, reeds, sedges, cattails, and grasses. They are wet areas which can be periodically covered by standing or slow-moving water and are usually associated with ponds, rivers, streams, inland lakes, and the Great Lakes. Although some marshes have sandy soils, marshes usually have finer textured, nutrient rich soils with large amounts of organic matter. There are many types of wetlands that are dominated by grasslike vegetation and

fall into the general category of marsh. One that deserves special note occurs in swales between beach ridges, wind blown depressions, and small embayments along the Great Lakes shoreline. These wetlands (referred to as interdunal swale

wetlands), depend on the Great Lakes for their water source. As such, their water table and period of saturation fluctuates with Great Lakes water levels. Because of the highly variable ecosystem characteristics, interdunal wetland/upland complexes support many endangered or threatened species such as the Piping Plover, Pitcher's thistle, Lake Huron tansy, or Houghton's goldenrod. Due to a combination of the natural fragility of interdunal wetlands and the loss of shoreline habitat due to development along the Great Lakes shoreline, these habitats are threatened.

Another type of marshlike wetland that deserves special note is the wet meadow. Wet meadows contain grasslike vegetation and contain saturated soils, but seldom have water standing on the ground surface. Many wet meadows occur in the former lake-plain of the Great Lakes, especially in southeast Michigan and the Saginaw Bay watershed. Accordingly, they are also referred to as lake-plain, or wet prairies. Because these areas are relics from a former geologic time, and a large percentage of these wetlands have been converted, they provide habitat for many plant species rare in Michigan that are typically adapted to prairies.

Marshes comprise the most biologically productive ecosystem in Michigan. The lush vegetation and rich invertebrate and insect life provide excellent habitat and breeding grounds for water birds such as ducks, geese, swans, and herons. The Common Loon, Bald Eagle, and Osprey also utilize marshes for feeding or nesting areas, as do numerous species of song birds. Marshes are also home to furbearing animals, such as muskrat and mink, and are important spawning grounds for many fish species.

Swamp

Swamps do not have the best public image. Movies like "The Swamp Thing" and place names like "The Great Dismal Swamp," convey a foreboding landscape. Swamps are simply wooded wetlands. Based on dominant vegetation, Michigan's swamps can generally be divided into three different types: a conifer swamp with trees such as tamarack, cedar, or balsam fir; a hardwood swamp with trees such as red maple, black ash, American elm, or balsam poplar; or a shrub swamp with shrubs such as tag alder, willows, or red osier dogwood.

Swamps are usually inundated or saturated periodically during the growing season. Some types of swamps, such as a red maple floodplain forest, are associated with lakes, rivers, or streams: others are associated with areas where the ground water is near the soil surface. The soils in swamps are usually rich in nutrients and organic matter. This is due to silt and organic matter deposited by flood events and the accumulation of organic matter (dead trees and other vegetation) over time.

The dense vegetation and proximity to surface water (especially along river systems) allow for high nutrient exchanges between land and water ecosystems. These factors contribute to the value of swamps as cover and food sources. Swamps provide very important habitat for a wide array of wildlife throughout the year, including deer, bear, raccoons, bobcats, songbirds, and many small animals.

Northern Peatland

Northern peatlands, commonly referred to as bogs, occur as thick peat deposits in old lake basins or as blankets of peat across the landscape. Their formation is due to the combination of cool temperatures and adequate rainfall in northern temperate regions around the earth which favor the accumulation of dead plant material. Michigan's peatlands are usually referred to as bogs or fens. In scientific terms, the main difference between a bog and a fen is based on the connection of the peatland to a source of ground water.

Bogs form in lake basins isolated from ground water (which generally contains minerals that reduce acidity). Because normal rain water (the only water source for true bogs) is slightly acidic, bog water tends to be slightly acidic. The acidic nature of bogs supports acid-loving (acidophilic) vegetation, especially sphagnum mosses, and contributes to a deficiency in available plant nutrients. As a result, many plants, animals, and microbes have special adaptations. An example of a unique adaptation can be found in vegetation such as the pitcher plant and sundew, which attain nutrients by catching and "digesting" insects. Other vegetation adapted to the highly acidic and nutrient poor conditions includes black spruce trees; shrubs such as leatherleaf, blueberries, and cranberries; and sedges such as cotton grass.

Although bogs can form in a number of ways, the most common in Michigan is the development of a "quaking bog." Typically, this successional process involves a small isolated lake basin (most likely a depression created when a large block of ice

melted after the glaciers retreated) that is gradually taken over by peat formed from the life and death of thousands of generations of plants growing on the edge of the basin. Since the production of plant material outstrips decomposition, the dead plants at the water's edge accumulate to form a floating mat of peat. Over many

thousands of years, a mat of mosses, reeds, sedges, grasses and other herbaceous plants develops along the leading edge of the floating mat. The older peat is then colonized by shrubs and eventually trees such as tamarack and spruce which form concentric rings around the advancing floating mat. When one ventures out onto this floating mat, the ground underfoot "quakes" with every step.

If a true bog is at one end of the northern peatland spectrum, then a calcareous (alkaline) fen is on the other. A calcareous fen (sometimes called a true fen) receives water that has passed through mineral soils rich in limestone. The ground cover in these peatlands is usually dominated by grasses, sedges, or reeds instead of sphagnum moss. On the peatland spectrum somewhere between a true bog and a true fen lies what is called a poor fen. Due to the accumulation of peat, a gradual reduction in ground water flow through the fen occurs. The resulting system is dominated by a combination of plants typically found in both bogs and fens, including sedges, sphagnum moss, leatherleaf, tamarack, bog laurel, bog birch, and other plant species typically associated with bogs like sundew and pitcher plants.

In general, northern peatlands provide valuable safety cover for many birds and animals. However, due to the low productivity and relative unpalatableness of bog vegetation, fens are generally more biologically productive than bogs.

WHY ARE WETLANDS IMPORTANT?

Wetlands are complex ecosystems that provide many ecological functions that are valued by society. In Michigan, these functions become increasingly significant as we continue to lose wetlands. The valuable ecological functions of wetlands and the aesthetically pleasing open space they provide help to enhance the quality of life for Michigan residents and visitors. When discussing the importance of wetlands, the terms "wetland functions" and "wetland values" are often used. Wetland

functions, such as sediment control and flood storage, are natural processes that continue regardless of their perceived value. Society does not necessarily attach value to all wetland functions. Value is usually associated with goods and services that wetlands provide. For this reason, wetland values, such as water quality maintenance and flood protection, are the goods and services that wetlands provide. Some common wetland functions and values are listed below.

Wetland Functions

Wetlands are known to be the most biological productive ecosystems in the temperate regions of the earth. Their biological productivity rivals that of tropical rainforests and involves complex nutrient and energy cycles. Many of the functions below are a direct result of the biological activity that occurs in wetlands.

Fish and Wildlife Habitat

Fish and wildlife habitat is the most widely celebrated and actively enjoyed wetland function. Many landowners own their wetlands solely for the benefits derived from this function. Some species spend their entire lives in wetlands, others utilize them intermittently for feeding or rearing their young. Simply put, wetlands provide critical habitat for Michigan's wildlife.

Most freshwater fish are considered wetland dependent. Fish feed in wetlands or on food produced there. Wetlands serve as nursery grounds for many species whose young take cover there, and many important sport fishes spawn in or near wetlands.

Like fish, many bird species are dependent on wetlands. Birds use wetlands for migratory resting places, breeding or feeding grounds, or taking cover from predators. It is estimated that over one-third of all bird species in North America rely on wetlands for one of these purposes.

Nearly all of Michigan's amphibians are wetland dependent, at least for breeding. Amphibians are sensitive to changes in wetland quality and quantity. Many scientists correlate declines in amphibian populations with wetland degradation worldwide.

Wetlands serve as the preferred habitat for many furbearing animals such as muskrat, beaver, otter, mink, and raccoon. In northern Michigan, cedar swamps are critical to white-tailed deer for many reasons, including winter browse (northern white cedar sustains deer in the absence of other foods) and important thermal cover during harsh winters.

Threatened and Endangered Species Habitat

Not surprisingly, wetland habitats are critical for the survival of threatened or endangered species. Endangered species are those that are in danger of becoming extinct. Threatened species are those that are in danger of becoming endangered. These species represent a unique element of Michigan's valuable natural heritage. More than one-third of all threatened or endangered animal species in the United States are either located in wetland areas or depend on them. This is especially critical considering that wetlands comprise only about five percent of the land mass of the lower 48 United States. Examples of Michigan's threatened or endangered animals that rely on wetlands include the Bald Eagle, Osprey, Common Loon, and King Rail. Of Michigan's total 395 threatened, endangered, rare, and special concern plant species, 194 of them are found in wetland habitats. Thus, nearly 50% of Michigan's plants of management concern reside in less than 15% percent of Michigan's surface area.

Water Pollution Control

A major function of wetlands is water quality protection. Wetlands function like living filters by removing polluting nutrients and sediments from surface and ground water. Although less well-known than providing fish and wildlife habitat, this wetland function is important to landowners and their communities.

Excess inputs of nutrients such as phosphorus and nitrogen can cause severe problems in aquatic ecosystems. You might say, "I thought nutrients were good." Nutrients such as phosphorus are necessary, but can be a classic example of how "too much of a good thing is bad." Excess nutrients can cause an undesirable increase in algae and aquatic plant growth. The result is water that is reminiscent of pea soup, weed-choked lakes, depleted dissolved oxygen levels, and the rapid aging or "eutrophication" of a lake. The massive algae blooms and depleted dissolved oxygen levels of Lake Erie in the early 1970's is a classic example of what happens to an aquatic system under the strain of too many nutrients.

Wetlands retain or remove nutrients in four ways: 1) uptake by plant life, 2) adsorption into sediments, 3) deposition of detritus (organic materials), and 4) chemical precipitation. The most significant of these are the uptake of nutrients by plants (which occurs primarily during the growing season, the same time that lakes and streams are most sensitive to nutrient inputs) and adsorption into sediments.

Sediment Control

As sediment-laden water flows through a wetland from the surrounding watershed, the sediments are deposited in the wetland. This reduces siltation into lakes, rivers, and streams. A combination of wetland vegetation and generally flat topography serves to slow water flow and increase deposition of silt and organic matter (carbon compounds). Because of the soil chemistry in wetlands, carbon compounds that are deposited in wetlands decompose very slowly. In this manner, wetlands serve as a relatively permanent resting place for carbon compounds. This function of wetlands can help to trap carbon that would otherwise accumulate in the upper atmosphere and contribute to global climate change. Furthermore, there is a strong tendency for heavy metals and other toxic chemicals to attach to the sediment particles found in surface water runoff. Wetlands can trap these human-induced pollutants and remove them from the water column. However, when the natural ability of wetlands to function as filters is overstressed from human inputs, the wetland and its functions can be destroyed. In fact, when overloaded, wetlands can actually become sources of pollutants, exporting materials that have been filtered and stored for centuries.

Water Supply

Wetlands are usually found where the ground water table intersects or is close to the land surface. Because of this, they are usually sites of ground water discharge. These sites are important for providing high quality water for our lakes, rivers, and streams. However, some wetlands are found where ground water recharge occurs. The recharge potential of a wetland varies according to a variety of factors, including wetland type, geographic location, subsurface geology, soil type, and precipitation.

Barrier to Waves and Erosion

In their natural condition, wetlands function as a barrier to erosion. The root systems of wetland plants stabilize soil at the water's edge and enhance soil accu-

mulation at the shoreline. Wetland vegetation along shorelines reduces erosion by dampening wave action and slowing current speed.

Flood Storage and Conveyance

Wetlands act as a hydrologic sponge, temporarily storing flood waters and releasing them slowly, thus reducing flood peaks and protecting downstream property owners from flood damage. Wetlands and adjacent floodplains often form natural floodways that convey flood waters from upland to downstream points. These functions become increasingly important in urban areas where development has increased the rate and volume of runoff.

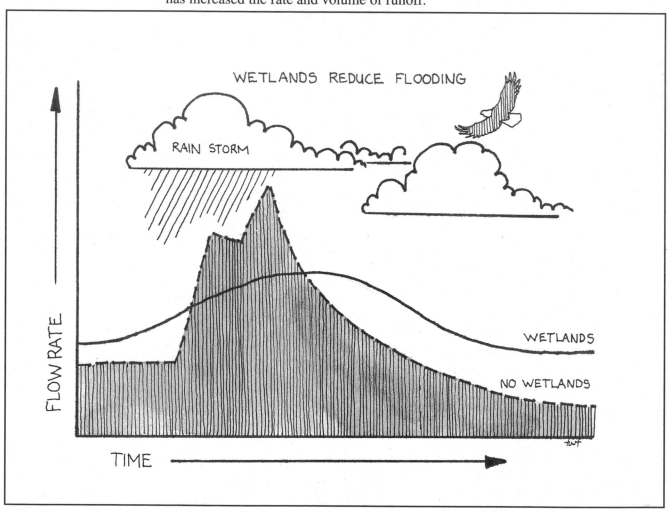

Wetland Values

Since practically every wetland function has some value to individuals and society, wetland values closely correspond to wetland functions.

Hunting, Fishing, and Trapping

Nationwide, over $10 billion is spent annually by an estimated 50 million people on fishing, hunting, and trapping. Since nearly all sport fish, many popular game animals, and most furbearing animals depend on wetlands for their survival, healthy and functioning wetland ecosystems are a necessity to maintain the resource base for this economy.

Water Quality Maintenance

Whether it is used for recreation, drinking water, or industrial processes, everyone needs clean water. On the delivery side of the water equation, clean water resulting from the water quality maintenance function of wetlands helps to keep water treatment costs low. Ground water is vulnerable to contamination at many recharge areas. The filtering capacity of wetlands and the absence of pollution-generating uses in wetlands serve to protect vulnerable aquifers. On the treatment side of the water use equation, the pollution treatment functions of natural wetlands have been mimicked in artificial wetlands constructed to serve as wastewater treatment systems and to reclaim areas degraded by strip mining. As alternatives to typical engineered systems, created wetlands provide a cost-effective way to meet human needs.

Water Supply

Because wetlands store water and slowly release it, they are often very important for maintaining base flow in streams. Wetlands are also very important for water storage during drought conditions. In severe drought years, the only vegetation lush enough to be cut for hay may be from wetland areas.

Food and Fiber Production

Wetlands support many commercial activities. In addition to the revenue generated by hunting, fishing, and trapping wetland species, wetlands provide a variety of natural products including blueberries, cranberries, and wild rice. Wetland grasses are cut for hay in many places for winter livestock feed. Forested wetlands, such as cedar swamps, can provide sustained yields of valuable timber if harvested with careful management and planning. It must be noted that many commercial activities, such as peat mining, logging, livestock grazing, or cranberry cultivation can severely degrade wetlands and a majority of their values if not done with the utmost of care.

Flood Protection

Each year, many Michigan communities experience severe flooding and millions of dollars in damage is caused by flooding across the United States. Due to below-market cost federal flood insurance and other forms of federal assistance to help flood victims, the American taxpayer bears a substantial portion of the financial burden of flood damage. The flood storage and conveyance functions of wetlands can help to prevent flooding, resulting in substantial savings to the taxpayer. In the late 1970's, the New England District of the United States Army Corps of Engineers concluded that natural wetland protection was the most cost effective means of floodwater control for the Charles River near Boston. As a result, they have acquired thousands of acres of wetlands in the Charles River watershed.

Erosion Control

Many riparian landowners experience erosion along the shore of their lake or stream. Often, this is a result of activities by the landowner that make the shoreline more susceptible to erosion (e.g., vegetation removal) or other human-caused circumstances (e.g., excessive boat waves). Vegetative erosion control, such as the establishment of wetland vegetation in the water and on the shoreline adjacent to the water can help to protect the property from erosion. Given the high market value of shoreline property, this wetland function is very important to riparian wetland property landowners.

Historic and Archeological Values

Some wetlands are important for historic, archeological, or paleontological reasons. Because wetlands served as a good source of food, early Native American settlements were often located in or near wetlands. Native American artifacts and well-preserved remains of prehistoric mammals have been found in wetlands.

Education and Research

Wetlands serve as wonderful outdoor classrooms, providing excellent living examples of nearly all components of ecology. Boardwalks and observation platforms have been constructed in many wetlands across the state to facilitate educational activities.

Recreation and Aesthetic Values

The richness of the plant and animal communities found in wetlands make them some of Michigan's most beautiful natural environments. Rare, threatened, and endangered plant and animal species provide added interest for naturalists. Wetlands provide valuable open space for visual and recreational enjoyment. In many cases throughout the state, protected wetlands have been shown to enhance the value of neighboring properties due to these factors. Perhaps the most valued function of wetlands is the space they provide for introspection and quiet reflection. The stresses of a busy day seem to fade away when one is watching a Great Blue Heron fishing in the marsh or admiring a delicate orchid in a bog.

Terms Used to Describe Wetlands

Over the thousands of years that people have been living with wetlands, many terms have been developed to describe them. Here are those that are common in the Midwest.

Aquatic Bed: Areas of shallow permanent water dominated by plants that grow on or below the surface of the water.

Bog: A peat-accumulating wetland that has no significant inflow or outflow of water and supports acidophilic vegetation, particularly sphagnum.

Bottomland: Lowlands (usually forested) along streams and rivers that are periodically flooded.

Fen: A peat-accumulating wetland that receives some water from surrounding mineral soils and usually supports grasslike vegetation.

Interdunal swale wetland: A wetland dominated by grasslike vegetation that occurs in the low areas between sand dunes or beach ridges along the Great Lakes shoreline.

Marsh: A frequently or continually inundated wetland characterized by grasslike and other emergent vegetation adapted to saturated soil conditions.

Muskeg: Large expanses of peatlands.

Peatland: A generic term for any peat-accumulating wetland.

Poor Fen: A peat-accumulating wetland that is transitional between a true bog and a true fen.

Pothole: A shallow pond dominated by grasslike vegetation.

Slough: A swamp or shallow lake system.

Swamp: A wetland dominated by trees or shrubs.

Wet meadow: Grassland with saturated soil near the surface but without standing water for most of the year.

Wet prairie: Intermediate between a marsh and a wet meadow.

Quantifying Wetland Values

Although it is obvious that wetlands are valuable, it is difficult to place a dollar value on the range of ecological functions that wetlands provide. This difficulty is due to many inherent problems associated with environmental economics, three of which are discussed below.

First, wetlands are valuable for many different reasons. Each wetland performs many different functions, the value of which often depends upon the person making the evaluation. Some functions are relatively easy to quantify (e.g., the value of the standing timber in a cedar swamp), while others are nearly impossible (e.g., the value of seeing a bobcat stalk a snowshoe hare in the same swamp). Complexity is added when one attempts to compare the value of the wetland in its natural state to the value of the wetland converted to a farm field or other non-wetland use.

Second, many wetland functions provide services that benefit the public as much (if not more) than the individual landowner. It is precisely because wetland functions are valued by society that regulations have been passed to protect them. However, some wetland functions, such as the flood storage capacity provided by a wetland located in the headwaters of a major river system, benefit downstream property owners more than the actual landowner. For another example, consider the

owner of a large marsh adjacent to a lake. The landowner does not economically benefit from the bass, pike, and other wetland-dependent fish that are caught in the lake by other anglers.

Third, and perhaps the most critical problem with attempting to quantify wetland values, is the issue of time frame. Wetlands provide ecological functions in perpetuity. Private entrepreneurs typically expect to recoup their investments within 10 to 30 years. Comparisons between short-term high economic yield projects and long-term ecological functions are inappropriate because economic analysis typically discounts the future value. Because of this, the decision regarding whether to convert a wetland (assuming the absence of regulations) will in the short term typically favor wetland destruction. It is important to remember that the destruction of wetlands by permanent conversion (e.g., house construction, filling, or draining) removes the ecological functions forever. On a related front, the economic evaluation of wetland conservation versus wetland conversion has an intergenerational

component. Future generations do not compete in the "marketplace," and therefore decisions that affect the natural resources that they will inherit are often made without their regard.

In summary, wetlands provide many ecological functions that are valuable to our quality of life, including recreational opportunities, flood storage, erosion control, and water quality maintenance. For many reasons, as with other natural resources, the monetary value of wetland functions is difficult to quantify. As we continue to lose wetlands, the functions that they provide will continue to increase in value. With the help of concerned wetland property owners like you, future generations will be able to experience (and surely find value in) the leap of a largemouth bass on the end of their line, abundant game in marshes and swamps across the state, and high quality water resources for a variety of uses.

Wetland Delineation: What You Need to Know

CHAPTER 3

DO I HAVE A WETLAND ON MY PROPERTY?

The answers to this question, and the obvious follow-up question ("If I do, then where are the wetland boundaries?"), have significant implications on property values, wildlife management activities, restoration and enhancement potential, and regulatory review. This chapter is designed to provide a general background regarding the science and practice of wetland determination and delineation. Knowing the basics about wetland delineation will help you understand and analyze the work of consultants and regulatory agency staff regarding wetland delineation. Furthermore, this information will allow you to be a careful and educated consumer when selecting a wetland consultant. It is important to note that wetland identification and delineation is a complicated process that requires substantial technical knowledge beyond what this chapter provides. For your own protection, hire a professional. Chapter 10 contains tips on how to select a wetland consultant.

Wetland determination (sometimes called identification) is simply the determination of whether an area is a wetland. Wetland delineation is the actual determination and establishment of wetland boundaries. For landowners who want to protect the natural resources on their property, just knowing that a wetland exists may be enough information for a hands-off form of stewardship. However, if you want to "do something" in or adjacent to your wetland that might impact the wetland's functions (or is a regulated activity), then knowing the wetland boundaries is essential.

On the state level, the Michigan Department of Environmental Quality (MDEQ) is responsible for determining wetland boundaries pursuant to Michigan's Wetland Protection statute. On the federal level, the U.S. Environmental Protection Agency (EPA), the U.S. Army Corps of Engineers (Corps), the U.S. Fish and Wildlife Service (FWS), and the Natural Resources Conservation Service (NRCS) all play a role in delineating wetlands in the administration of Federal law that

Where Are Wetlands Usually Found?

Wetlands are typically found in depressions, the lowest portion of the landscape, or adjacent to lakes, rivers, or streams. Landscape position, climate, and soil type all influence wetland formation. You can expect to find wetlands in the following places:

- In low areas with a high water table.
- On slopes where groundwater breaks out as springs or seeps.
- Near rivers, streams, lakes, and the Great Lakes.
- In flat areas where clayey soils or bedrock close to the surface form an impervious layer that creates a "perched" water table.
- In abandoned ditches or stream channels.

addresses wetlands (both for incentive programs and regulations). For the purposes of this document, the discussion here will focus on wetland determination and delineation procedures used by the MDEQ.

Currently, the Michigan Department of Environmental Quality delineates wetlands according to The Michigan Department of Natural Resources *Wetland Determination Draft Manual for Field Testing*. The purpose of this manual is to formalize the process used to delineate wetlands as they are defined by state law:

> "Wetland" means land characterized by the presence of water at a frequency and duration sufficient to support, and that under normal circumstances does support, wetland vegetation or aquatic life, and is commonly referred to as a bog, swamp, or marsh.
> [Section 30301(d), Part 303, Wetland Protection Act 451 of 1994]

Translating this statutory definition to an actual wetland delineation involves investigating vegetation communities and hydrology. Under Michigan's delineation methodology, soils are used as an indicator of hydrology. According to state law, all local units of government in Michigan must use the MDEQ's definition of wetlands. Federal wetland definitions and delineation methods differ slightly from state law. The primary difference between state and federal wetland delineation methods is that the federal delineation method considers hydric soils to be a separate required parameter on its own instead of an indicator of wetland hydrology.

Although regulatory definitions and delineation methods among agencies and those used by consultants are essentially the same, the actual "line" between upland and wetland is

Do I Have A Wetland On My Property?

Many property owners are confused about the technical definitions of wetlands. This is understandable given the variety of wetlands in Michigan and the fact that many wetland types look different than our traditional conception of a wetland (which is typically a cattail marsh). Below are a few questions that you can ask yourself about your land that relate to the information in this chapter. A YES answer to any of the questions may indicate that you have a wetland on your property.

YES	NO	
☐	☐	Is the ground soggy underfoot in the spring?
☐	☐	Are there depressions where water pools on the ground surface during the spring?
☐	☐	Do you avoid the area with heavy equipment for fear of getting stuck?
☐	☐	Would you need to ditch the site to dry it out?
☐	☐	Is the site in a depression that has a different vegetation community than the higher ground around it?
☐	☐	Are there groundwater seeps or springs present?
☐	☐	Are fallen leaves black or very darkly stained and contain sediment deposits on their surfaces?
☐	☐	Dig a hole. Is the soil gray, or contain bright mottles (red or orange) against a gray background?
☐	☐	If farmed, is there crop stress due to excessive water?
☐	☐	Does the National Wetland Inventory map, U.S.G.S. topographical map, or locally produced wetland inventory map show a wetland on your property?
☐	☐	Does the NRCS Soil Survey for your county show the soil on your property to be hydric, poorly, or very poorly drained?

not always clear. This is understandable when you consider the variety of wetlands that occur in Michigan and that wetlands are ecosystems subject to natural influences that fluctuate (e.g., rainfall, temperature, or lake levels). State and federal agency staff sometimes disagree slightly on wetland boundaries. In addition, agency staff sometimes disagree with delineations conducted by consultants. Often, the resolution of disputed wetland boundaries requires multiple site visits with both parties. It is important to remember that the state and federal regulatory agencies have the ultimate authority over boundaries of wetlands regulated by state and federal statute.

ENVIRONMENTAL INDICATORS OF WETLANDS

According to Michigan's wetland delineation methods, there are two primary indicators of wetlands:

1) The predominance of plants adapted for living in saturated conditions (hydrophytic, or wetland, vegetation); and

2) The presence of water at or near the land surface throughout the year or for some portion of the year (wetland hydrology), which is commonly indicated by the presence of distinctive soils that develop under saturated conditions (hydric soils).

These indicators are interrelated, and with few exceptions, are present in undisturbed wetland areas. A 1995 report by the National Academy of Sciences reaffirms the scientific validity of wetland delineation methods that investigate vegetation, hydrology, and soils (either separately or as an indicator of hydrology). These indicators are briefly described below.

What's A Wetland Indicator Status?

The U.S. Fish and Wildlife Service, in cooperation with other agencies and professional botanists, developed the following categories to help determine if a vegetation community would be considered to be adapted to wetland conditions:

Obligate wetland plants (OBL)—Species in this category are estimated to occur in wetlands more than 99 percent of the time.

Facultative wetland plants (FACW)— Species in this category are estimated to occur in wetlands approximately 67-99 percent of the time.

Facultative plants (FAC)—Species in this category are estimated to occur in wetlands approximately 34-66 percent of the time.

Not Shown:

Facultative upland plants (FACU)—Species in this category are estimated to occur in wetlands approximately 1-33 percent of the time.

Obligate upland plants (UPL)—Species in this category are estimated to occur in wetlands less than 1 percent of the time.

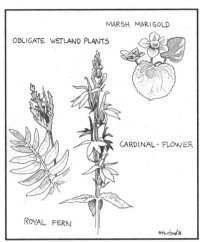

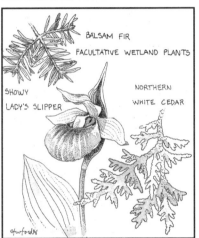

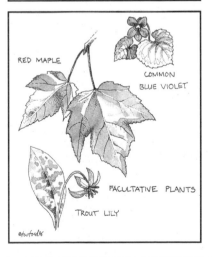

Hydrophytic Vegetation

Hydrophytic (water-loving, or wetland) vegetation is plant life that is adapted to grow in areas where the frequency and duration of inundation or saturation is sufficient to exert a controlling influence over the plant species present. Among other things, all plants need oxygen and water. There is a point at which the frequency and duration of water in the soil causes at least periodic deficiencies in oxygen in the root zone. This is because water replaces air in the spaces between the soil particles in saturated conditions. In order to survive the stress of low

oxygen levels in the root zone, hydrophytic plants have structural and functional adaptations to allow them to thrive in these areas. As a result, they out compete other plants that are not adapted to living in saturated conditions. An example of a common adaptation that allows wetland plants to survive in wet conditions can be easily observed by cutting a cattail near its base. The air-filled tissue that you see in the cross-section transports air to the roots of the plant so that it can live in inundated areas.

For the wetland plant criteria to be met in determining that an area is a wetland, a predominance of wetland vegetation must be present—not just the occurrence of a single wetland plant. In other words, a wetland will have a community of plants that are adapted to survive in wet conditions. To help wetland delineators determine if a plant community is adapted to wetland conditions, the U.S. Fish and Wildlife Service (in cooperation with the Corps, the EPA, and the NRCS) has published a list of plant species that occur in wetlands for each state and region. The list separates plants into five basic groups, ranging from plants which almost always occur in wetlands to plants which almost never occur in wetlands. These five categories are referred to as wetland indicator statuses or wetland fidelity ratings. Typically, an area is considered to have a wetland plant community when more than 50 percent of the dominant species in each layer of vegetation (e.g., tree layer, shrub layer, or herb layer) have wetland indicator statuses of FAC, FACW, or OBL (see side-bar for wetland indicator status definitions).

Common Field Indicators of Wetland Hydrology

In the absence of hydrologic data or direct evidence of hydrology, the following field indicators can be used to assess wetland hydrology.

Oxidized root channels: Some hydrophytic plants transport oxygen to their root zone. Although iron in anaerobic environments is usually in a reduced state, the oxygen that is transported through the root channels causes it to oxidize (rust) along the root or rhizome and form iron oxide concretions (orange or red-brown in color) along the length of the root channel.

Water marks: Water marks are commonly found on woody vegetation. They often occur as stains on bark or other fixed objects such as bridges or pilings. Plants and other vertical objects often have thin layers, coatings, or depositions of mineral or organic matter after inundation.

Drift lines: Drift lines consist of debris (remnants of vegetation, sediment, litter, etc.) that was deposited as a result of water movement. Most common adjacent to streams or other sources of water flow, debris is usually deposited parallel to the direction of water flow. However, because shallow water can extend beyond where the debris is deposited, drift lines do not represent the maximum level of inundation.

Water-stained leaves: Forested wetlands that are inundated earlier in the year will frequently have water-stained leaves on the forest floor. These leaves are generally grayish or blackish in appearance from being underwater for significant periods and are typically coated with sediment.

Surface scoured areas: Surface scouring occurs along floodplains where overbank flooding erodes sediments. The absence of leaf litter from the soil surface is also sometimes an indication of prolonged duration.

Wetland Hydrology

Wetland hydrology refers to the specific hydrologic conditions that are required to form and maintain wetlands. Saturation at or near the surface, or inundation, for approximately 14 days or more during Michigan's growing season typically creates the necessary conditions in the soil to form and maintain wetlands. Wetland hydrology, hydric soils, and hydrophytic vegetation are all linked. Hydrophytic vegetation and hydric soils result from wetland hydrology; and conversely, the presence of hydrophytic vegetation and hydric soils indicate wetland hydrology.

Of the indicators used for wetland identification, wetland hydrology is the most variable and often the most difficult to observe directly. Numerous factors influence hydrology, including time of year, precipitation, topography, soil permeability, and plant cover. The technical wetland hydrology criteria looks at the distance to the water table based on soil drainage and permeability characteristics. Depending on the soil series, an area can have wetland hydrology even if the ground surface is never covered with water, so long as the water table is close enough to the surface to influence the root zone and cause the development of a wetland plant community.

Evidence of wetland hydrology can come from a variety of sources. When available, recorded hydrologic data or aerial photographs can be useful. Perhaps the best evidence is the direct visual observation of inundation or soil saturation. Saturated soils may be detected by digging a hole at least 18 inches deep and observing the water table after it has had a chance to stabilize in the hole.

In the absence of reliable hydrologic data or direct evidence of hydrology, field indicators have been developed for assessing wetland hydrology. These indicators are useful during the drier portions of the growing season when visual evidence of inundation or saturation is not possible. Some of the most common field indicators for hydrology include oxidized root channels, water marks, or surface scoured areas. Under Michigan's wetland delineation method, perhaps the most useful hydrology indicator is the presence of a hydric soil.

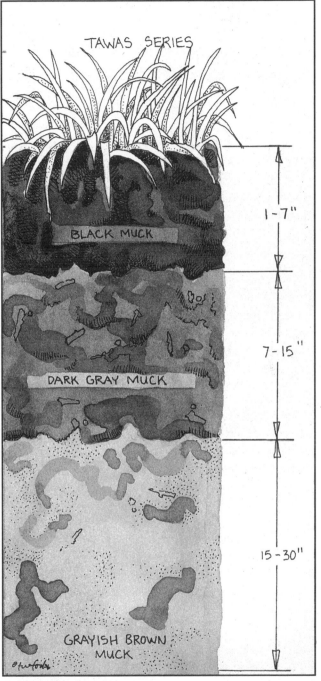

Hydric Soils

Hydric soils have physical and chemical indicators of repeated and prolonged saturation at or near the soil surface. These indicators are a direct result of the lack of oxygen in the upper part of the soil caused by the presence of water in the spaces between soil particles (which forces air out of the soil). In Michigan and most of the temperate regions of the United States, hydric soils are flooded, ponded, or saturated for about 14 or more days during the growing season.

The U.S. Department of Agriculture has developed a basic system of soil classification. There have been 10,500 types of soils, called soils series, identified in the United States. Hydric soils are usually divided into two categories: organic and mineral. Organic soils are so named because they are made up of partly decomposed organic matter that forms peats and mucks. Almost all organic soils are considered hydric soils. The mineral soils that are hydric are set apart from other mineral soils because of their poor drainage characteristics or susceptibility to ponding and flooding. Because of these features, there is often a layer of muck

that forms above the mineral component of the soil. There are several field indicators that can help in determining if a soil would be considered hydric, including organic surface layers, sulfitic materials, and soil color.

The National Technical Committee for Hydric Soils has developed criteria for hydric soils as well as a list of the nation's hydric soils, of which there are approximately 2,100 in the United States. Sometimes, a list of hydric soils is developed locally for individual counties. Generally, the county list is more reliable due to recent updating and local knowledge.

Field Indicators of Hydric Soils

There are several field indicators that can help in determining if a soil would be considered hydric, including:

Organic Soils: Are easily recognized as thick peats and mucks. Mucks feel greasy when rubbed between the fingers. Partially decomposed plant remains can be identified in peats.

Organic Surface Layer: Organic surface layers often form above the mineral substrate in hydric mineral soils due to the greatly slowed decomposition of the organic matter as a result of soil saturation and inundation.

Sulfidic Material: Soils that emit an odor of rotten eggs indicate permanent saturation and the presence of sulfidic material. Such permanent saturation causes anaerobic conditions that cause the sulfidic material to be chemically reduced to form hydrogen sulfide.

Soil Color: Due to the presence of water in the soil column creating very low oxygen conditions, hydric mineral soils often form diagnostic colors. The two main categories of hydric soil colors are gleyed and low chroma/mottled soils. Gleying (bluish, greenish, or grayish colors) is an indication of a soil that is saturated for prolonged periods. Low chroma (dull) colors and mottles (bright splotches of color in a dull matrix) indicate soils that are alternately saturated and unsaturated during the growing season. Accurately identifying soil colors usually requires comparing the soil to standardized color charts made specifically for that purpose.

Dark Vertical Streaking: In sandy soils with an organic surface layer, organic matter is moved downward through the sand as the water table fluctuates. This often occurs more rapidly in some sections of the soil than in others. As a result, a cross-sectional view of the soil as revealed in a soil pit will appear to be vertically streaked. (It is important to note that some non-hydric soils may also reveal vertical streaking.)

Iron and Manganese Concretions: Under the chemical conditions of hydric soils, iron and manganese are sometimes segregated into concretions or soft masses. These accumulations are usually black or dark brown.

EXCEPTIONS

Although these indicators are routinely used by consultants and agency staff, it is important to note that there are several situations in which wetlands will not show direct evidence of these indicators. These areas include wetlands that have been disturbed (human intervention may have removed one or more of the indicators), newly created wetlands (hydric soils or hydrophytic vegetation may not have had a chance to fully develop), interdunal swale wetlands (hydric soils or wetland hydrology may be difficult to identify), and wetlands on sloping glacial till (wetland hydrology may not be evident). In addition, there are some cases in which wetlands can become dominated by facultative upland species. Although this is not a comprehensive list, it does provide examples of situations where the basic indicators of wetlands would not be readily evident.

CONCLUSION

As you can see by this condensed description of the basics, the scientific basis for wetland delineation is quite complicated. If nothing else, what you need to know about wetland identification and delineation can be summed up like this: Land does not need to be wet all year to be a wetland—it only needs to be wet long enough during the growing season to exert a controlling influence on the vegetation so that a wetland plant community occurs there.

This chapter is not meant to serve as a wetland delineation manual. Rather, its purpose is to provide you with enough information to understand the scientific basis for wetland determination and delineation. This information will help you select a wetland consultant who will meet your needs and help you understand wetland determinations and delineations conducted on your property. To become more familiar with the indicators of wetlands, take some time to explore your wetland and investigate the soils, plants, and hydrology. Chapter 4 provides some suggestions to get you started exploring and assessing your wetland.

Wetland Identification Resources

There are many available resources for landowners who want to know as much as possible about the wetlands on their property. Although many of these resources are referred to as "wetland maps," it is important to note that most are developed from "off-site" information and none of them provide definitive wetland boundaries. There is simply no substitute for on-site wetland delineation conducted by a trained professional.

Natural Resource Conservation Service Soil Surveys: The U.S. Department of Agriculture's Natural Resource Conservation Service (NRCS) has conducted surveys of the soils in most counties of the state. The soil surveys contain a wealth of useful information, including soil maps, engineering suitability ratings, soil profile descriptions, and hydrologic characteristics. This information is extremely valuable in determining if a hydric soil occurs on a site. Keep in mind, however, that soil survey maps are not accurate enough to show the exact boundaries of a soil series. For this reason, it's always advisable to dig a soil pit and compare what you see to the soil description. Soil surveys are available from your county Soil and Water Conservation District, or your NRCS District Conservationist.

Hydric Soils of the State of Michigan: The Natural Resources Conservation Service, in cooperation with the National Technical Committee for Hydric Soils, has compiled a list of hydric soils in Michigan. This list can be used in conjunction with county soil surveys to locate areas where wetlands might occur. This publication is available from your county Soil and Water Conservation District, or your NRCS District Conservationist.

Michigan Resource Information System (MIRIS) Current Use Inventory Maps: These maps are compiled by the Michigan Inventory Program of the Michigan Department of Natural Resources. The maps contain inventories of 60 different land use classifications of which approximately 12 relate to wetlands. Specific classes of wetlands include wooded, shrub swamp, aquatic bed, emergent, and mud flats. In addition, there are other classes which are not classified as wetland in the MIRIS system, but more than likely would be considered jurisdictional wetlands. These include lowland hardwood and lowland conifer forest classifications. The wetland boundaries shown on these maps are meant to identify approximate boundaries. To find out if your county has a completed MIRIS inventory, call your county planning and zoning department or regional planning office.

National Wetlands Inventory (NWI) Maps: On these maps, wetlands are delineated based on features shown on aerial photographs and are usually displayed on USGS topographic maps. NWI maps are used to show the approximate extent of a wetland and its association with other wetland and non-wetland areas. Due to the scale of the aerial photography used and the lack of ground verification, NWI maps cannot be used as the sole basis for determining whether an area is a wetland. To order NWI Maps, contact the MSU Distribution Center, 104 Central Services, E. Lansing, MI, 48824-1001; or call (517) 353-6740.

United States Geological Survey (USGS) Topographic Maps: These maps are available in several different scales and provide landmark features including towns, roads, bridges, streams, buildings, water bodies, etc. that are not found commonly on road maps. The topographic lines and elevations are helpful in determining drainage patterns. These maps should not be used to delineate wetland boundaries, as the scale

Wetland Identification Resources, continued

is too small to make the boundaries accurate, and not all wetlands are indicated. However, those areas that are marked as wetlands are most likely to be wetlands unless altered since the map was made. To order USGS Topo Maps, call 1-800-USA-MAPS.

Natural Resource Conservation Service Mapping: As part of their administrative responsibilities under the conservation provisions of the Farm Bill, the NRCS maps wetlands on agricultural lands enrolled in agricultural conservation programs. Although NRCS maps do not define jurisdiction for wetland permitting under Michigan's law, they can provide useful information. The Farmed Wetland and Prior Converted mapping classifications can be especially helpful in identifying wetland restoration and enhancement sites. Contact your NRCS District Conservationist to see if these maps are available for your property.

Local Wetlands Maps and Inventories: Many local organizations or municipal governments have developed wetland maps for their service area. Although they vary greatly in terms of scale and quality, they can serve as excellent resources.

Wetland Plants of the State of Michigan: The U.S. Fish and Wildlife Service, as part of the National Wetlands Inventory Program, has compiled a wetland plant list for Michigan. This plant list includes a comprehensive list of the plants that occur in wetlands, including their wetland indicator status. This plant list is essential for determining if an area meets wetland vegetation criteria. To order this publication, contact the U.S. Fish and Wildlife Service Field Office in Lansing.

Plant Identification Guidebooks: The precise identification of vegetation to the species level is necessary to determine if an area has a hydrophytic vegetation community. For example, identifying a tree as a "maple" is not very helpful, as there are six species of the maple family in Michigan, with wetland indicator statuses ranging from FACW to FACU. There are numerous excellent plant guidebooks to choose from, including *Michigan Trees* by Barnes and Wagner, *Ferns of Michigan* by Billington, *Michigan Wildflowers* by Smith, and *Michigan Flora* by Voss. In addition, there are several guidebooks specific to wetland plants.

Aerial Photography: Although not as readily available to the public as the sources listed above, aerial photography or other remote sensing data can be very helpful. Aerial photography can be particularly useful in identifying patterns of plant communities.

Local Knowledge: In addition to these published resources, information about the wetlands on your property may be available from former landowners or long-time residents of your area.

Exploring and Assessing Your Wetland

Every wetland is unique. The more you explore your wetland, the more you will understand its unique character. What wildlife live in your wetland? What vegetation communities exist there? How are the soils different than those in the uplands? How far below the surface is the water table in the summer? How does the wetland fit into the watershed? By knowing the answers to these questions, you will increase your enjoyment of your wetland and gain information that will be useful when planning management activities. As you learn more about your wetland, you may want to share your knowledge with others. The exploration methods described below can be made into enjoyable activities that can bring your family closer together. You might also want to share your wetland knowledge with local teachers or school groups. Children are fascinated by the rich life found in wetlands.

It is important, however, to remind ourselves that overuse of an area can result in a reduction of its ecological functions. You surely don't want to "love it to death." For example, intense human use of an area may adversely impact use of the area by wildlife. By using caution and being sensitive to disturbing vegetation and wildlife, you will increase your overall enjoyment of the area. The information here is supplemental to Chapter 3. As such, many of the wetland identification resources mentioned in Chapter 3 would prove useful here.

WILDLIFE

Providing wildlife habitat is one of the most important wetland functions. The diversity of habitat types found within wetlands makes them attractive to more species of wildlife than any other ecosystem type. Wetland property owners are blessed with sights and sounds that most people do not have the opportunity to experience: a mallard duck herding her ducklings into the cattails, the chorus of spring peepers ushering in an April twilight, or the snakelike movements of a hunting mink.

Observing wildlife and making a list of species that you see or hear is a great way to start exploring your wetland. All you'll need is a pencil and note pad; clothes appropriate for weather, wetness conditions, and biting insects (not all wetland animals are cute and cuddly!); a pair of binoculars; a few field guides; and some time. Perhaps the most important item on this list is time. Like hunting, successful wildlife observation requires us to take enough time to become part of the landscape. When we quietly fade into the background of the wetland, the wildlife suddenly emerge and we are given front-row seats to experience the drama of nature.

Your list of wildlife species should include the date and time of day the animal was seen and the number of individuals observed. Although the hour before sunset and the hour after sunrise are considered "magic hours" for wildlife observation, you might find it interesting to observe wildlife at different times of the day. Ideally, you will be able to observe your wetland throughout the year. This way you'll be able to discover what different animals use the wetland during different seasons. In addition to the names of animals, you can include notes on what the animals are doing. Are they building nests, foraging for food, or interacting with other animals? Don't forget to include frogs, butterflies, and other smaller creatures on your wildlife list. Often we overlook these animals for more charismatic fauna, but they too can be very interesting and entertaining to observe with our eyes and ears.

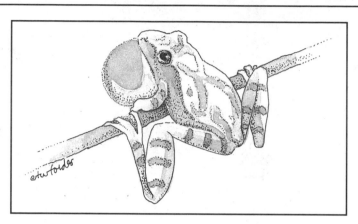

Frog and Toad Surveys

If you are interested in exploring the frogs and toads that use your wetland, the Michigan Department of Natural Resources (MDNR) Natural Heritage Program is coordinating a statewide Frog and Toad Survey program. This innovative program was initiated in response to a growing awareness and concern about globally declining amphibian populations. The objective is to monitor statewide the long-term population trends of native species of frogs and toads.

Those who participate in the program are provided with a tape recording that identifies the calls of native frog and toad species. A survey route consisting of 10 sites in wetlands is established and is monitored three times during the amphibians' breeding season, which is generally between April and early to mid-July (exact times vary from year to year, and depend on the location within the state). Participants record weather conditions, water temperatures, and after listening at each site for 3-5 minutes, a call index for each species heard. The call index provides a measurement of the abundance of each identified species.

If you are interested in participating in the statewide Frog and Toad Survey as part of learning more about your wetland, contact:

Wildlife Division
Michigan Department of Natural Resources
Natural Heritage Program
P.O. Box 30180
Lansing, MI 48909
PH (517) 373-9418

A special note should be made regarding threatened and endangered species. Because of the unique habitat that wetlands provide, and the large percentage of wetlands that have been lost in Michigan, wetlands provide habitat for many threatened and endangered animal species. Landowners that have threatened and endangered species on their property are very fortunate to have the opportunity to preserve an important piece of Michigan's natural heritage. If you think that you may have threatened or endangered animals on your property, contact the Michigan

Natural Heritage Program, Wildlife Division, Michigan Department of Natural Resources or the U.S. Fish and Wildlife Service Field Office in East Lansing. Agency staff can provide information and help develop management plans to protect these valuable species.

Your list doesn't need to be limited to animals that you actually see or hear. Keep lists of *signs* of wildlife as well. Animal tracks, bird nests, feathers or hair, and scat (droppings) also should be included in the list since it may be difficult to view many of the wildlife species that use your wetland. You may consider putting in a viewing blind where you can sit quietly and wait for wildlife to appear. Your blind should be made in a way that it blends into its surroundings. Volunteer wetland monitoring programs such as the MDNR's Frog and Toad Survey and the Marsh Monitoring Program developed at the Long Point Observatory in Ontario employ a "route" that is consistently walked at specific times to observe wildlife. This is a good way to get consistent observations of wildlife in your wetland in a way that allows you to objectively compare observation visits. When setting up your own route, try to make

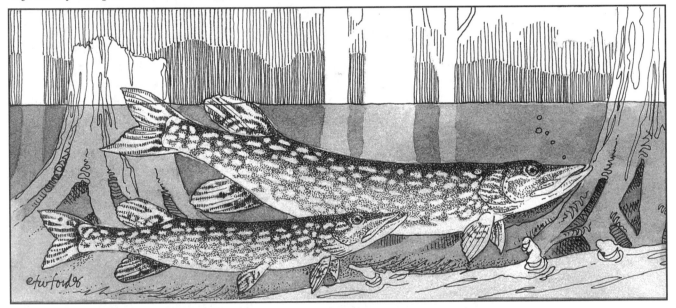

sure that you cover each different habitat type in your wetland and locate the best route to ensure that important habitat or sensitive vegetation communities do not become trampled.

Because you can use your ears to "see" them, birds can be especially interesting to observe. Find a spot to sit comfortably and quietly, close your eyes, and listen. As the echoes of the farm machinery, office, or job site fade from your ears, how many different bird sounds do you hear? Can you envision the birds making the calls? Can you identify the different birds by only their song? Do not be discouraged if you cannot identify all the bird calls. There are many bird call training tapes available from mail order catalogs, wild bird specialty shops, and organizations such as the National Audubon Society. When you learn bird calls, you will be amazed at how much more you hear when you are in your wetland. If you find that birding really appeals to you, you might want to participate in the annual breeding bird survey. For information, contact your local Audubon Society chapter.

If you have permanent open water in your wetland, or your wetland is adjacent to a lake or stream, then fish may be an important component of the wildlife that you can observe. Most fish in Michigan utilize wetlands for some portion of their life cycle and they are a very important part of the food chain for other animals. Your ability to observe fish will depend on a variety of factors, including time of year, clarity of water, accessibility, species of fish using the wetland, and glare from sunlight off the water. Perhaps the most exciting time of the year to observe fish in

wetlands is during the spring spawning season. In some parts of Michigan, northern pike spawn in flooded swamps. Other large fish such as largemouth bass, long-nosed gar, and carp spawn in or near marshes. During daylight hours, observation can be enhanced by wearing polarized lenses. Since many large fish are most active during the night, a spotlight and a rowboat can be a very effective combination for seeing fish spawning and feeding in wetlands.

Get Involved in Statewide Bird Surveys!

Michigan Audubon Society (MAS), the state's oldest conservation organization, annually seeks new and continuing volunteers to participate in two ongoing bird surveys:

MAS Winter Bird Feeder Survey

Each winter, hundreds of Michigan naturalists count the various species of birds visiting their feeders. Participants in the survey count the maximum number of species they observe at their feeder location at any one time on one day during the months of November through April.

MAS Seasonal Bird Survey

This annual survey is a tradition spanning more than 70 years. It allows individuals to participate to the level and degree that they choose. You can cover as much area or as little as you like. Survey birds regularly or infrequently. Count all species observed or just those that interest you.

The goal of both surveys is to determine and document changes in the seasonal distribution and abundance of Michigan's bird populations and to monitor their long-term population fluctuations.

If you would like to participate, contact:

MAS Winter Bird Feeder Survey
Kalamazoo Nature Center
7000 N. Westnedge Ave.
Kalamazoo, MI 49004
(616) 381-1574

MAS Seasonal Bird Survey
6011 W. St. Joseph Hwy., Suite 403
P.O. Box 80527
Lansing, MI 48908-0527
(517) 886-9144

VEGETATION

Although hydrologic characteristics determine many features of wetland ecosystems, the types of plants that grow in a wetland greatly influence the habitat for wildlife and play a critical role in such important wetland functions as flood storage and water quality protection by nutrient and sediment retention. There are several different ways to explore and assess wetland vegetation in your wetland.

Species Diversity

One reason why wetlands provide excellent wildlife habitat is because many different plants grow there. Making a plant list is probably the simplest way to explore the plant diversity of your wetland. Like the wildlife list, keep track of the plants you see as you visit your wetland. If you can't identify a specific plant, make a sketch of it and note some of its characteristics so you can include it in the list and identify it later. Some identifying characteristics include flower type and color, height, leaf shape, and whether it is woody. There are many very useful plant identification guides that will help you to identify Michigan's plants. Some of them have step-wise keys that lead you through a process to help you identify a particular plant. If you've never used a plant key before, it's helpful to practice working through and getting comfortable with the key by "identifying" plants that you already know.

In scientific terms, diversity is a single measure with two different components: the number of species (termed richness); and the distribution of individuals among species (termed evenness). In simple terms, a truly diverse vegetation community has a lot of different species and the individual populations of each species are fairly even. So, in addition to simply listing the species, it is often helpful to quantify how many of each species there are in a given area. There are many ways to do this, ranging from counting individual plants to estimating percent aerial cover. When you determine the relative abundance of each of the plant species present, you can then determine the dominant plant species. Dominant species are those which, when ranked in descending order of their abundance and cumulatively totaled, exceed 50 percent of the total, plus any species comprising 20 percent or more of the total. Knowing the dominant plant species is helpful when characterizing a wetland. For example, a swamp is typically identified by its dominant plant species (e.g., a red-maple swamp or a lowland conifer swamp where cedar and balsam fir are dominant).

It might be interesting to compare the diversity of plant life in a wetland to other areas on your property. One way to do this is to count herbaceous plant stems in randomly located equal-sized plots. The simplest way to do this is to build a wooden frame or hoop of plastic tubing (of a manageable size—approximately one

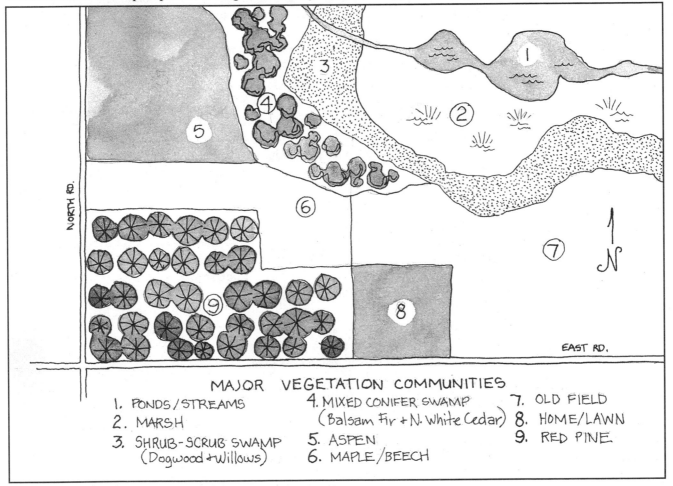

NORTH RD.

EAST RD.

MAJOR VEGETATION COMMUNITIES
1. PONDS / STREAMS
2. MARSH
3. SHRUB-SCRUB SWAMP (Dogwood + Willows)
4. MIXED CONIFER SWAMP (Balsam Fir + N. White Cedar)
5. ASPEN
6. MAPLE / BEECH
7. OLD FIELD
8. HOME / LAWN
9. RED PINE

square meter) to be placed on the ground in different habitats. Randomly place the frame or hoop anywhere in your wetland, and count the numbers of different plants you find there. It is not necessary to identify the plants, just note the number of different species and how many of each there are. Do this in several locations throughout the wetland. Take the same frame and do the same tests in other surroundings (e.g., upland forest, old field, etc). Although there are some types of wetlands where this sort of analysis will not work well (e.g., a monotypical cattail stand or the understory of a densely shaded swamp where not much grows on the ground), most of the time you should find there is more diversity in the wetland.

Vegetation Communities

As you investigate the vegetation in your wetland, you will notice that certain species of plants are located in discrete locations and are usually found in association with certain other plant species. These associations of plants are referred to as communities. Plant communities reflect a variety of factors: soils, water table depth, water quality, characteristics of adjacent water bodies, slope, aspect, and adjacent land use. Sometimes these vegetation communities are distinct (such as a

shrub swamp alongside a marsh). Other times they are harder to identify. As you become more familiar with the types of vegetation in your wetland, you will start to understand the underlying reasons for each of the communities. For example, you may note that the tag alders and willows only grow in soil that is saturated to the surface all year, whereas the cedars grow on somewhat higher and dryer sites.

To visualize the "big picture" of the vegetation in your wetland, it is helpful to map the various vegetation communities. This can be done by making a simple sketch of your wetland which indicates where the vegetation changes occur. A more detailed map can be developed by walking transects and indicating the precise distances from a base line where each vegetation community change occurs. The distances are then translated onto a scaled map. No matter how you make your vegetation community map, the key to a good one is that it provides a reasonable representation of the vegetation communities in your wetland. A map of the vegetation communities provides useful information regarding the diversity of wildlife habitat that your wetland provides. In addition, plant community diversity (also called interspersion) can be important with respect to water quality and flood storage. Different plant communities slow water and uptake nutrients in different ways. Areas with a diversity of plant communities are able to take advantage of the differences in how each plant community functions. As a result, the entire wetland provides flood storage and water quality maintenance functions in a more comprehensive manner.

As noted in Chapter 2, Michigan's wetlands provide habitat for more than half of Michigan's rare, threatened, or endangered plant species. As with threatened and endangered animal species, landowners who have threatened or endangered plants on their property have a unique opportunity to be stewards of a very rare resource. If you think you may have threatened or endangered plants on your property, contact the Michigan Natural Heritage Program, Wildlife Division, Michigan Department of Natural Resources or the U.S. Fish and Wildlife Service Field Office in East Lansing. Agency staff can provide information and help develop management plans to protect these valuable species.

WETLANDS AND WATERSHEDS

A watershed (also called a drainage basin) is the geographic area that drains to a single water body. A large watershed, such as that for Saginaw Bay, is made up of many smaller watersheds (e.g., Saginaw River, Tittabawassee River, etc.). How your wetland is situated in the watershed influences its function. Understanding what lands drain to the wetland and how the wetland fits into the larger scheme of the watershed is important to the landowner.

Determining what lands drain to your wetland is a fairly simple process. A good 7.5-minute topographic map (1:25,000 scale) and your own knowledge of the watershed are all it takes.

Once you have the topographic (topo for short) map(s) for your area, find the location of your wetland on the map. In most cases the wetland will be at a low elevation and the land surrounding it will rise (the numbers on the lines of the topographic map will increase as you go away from your wetland). Because topographic maps only have general wetland boundaries identified, you might need to consult some of the other resources listed in Chapter 3 (e.g., NWI Map) to better determine the size and shape of your wetland. Now, draw a line on the map that encompasses all the lands that "shed" water to your wetland. One way to do this involves starting at the north end of your wetland and, moving northerly, follow the rising topography lines until you reach the spot where the land elevation is the greatest. The highest elevation point marks the edge of the wetland's watershed in this direction. The water that falls on land north of this spot will flow away from your wetland; that which falls south of it will flow toward your wetland. Use this same exercise to mark the southern, eastern, and western boundaries of the watershed. Keep repeating this procedure in different directions from your wetland until the dots on the topographic map start to reveal the watershed. Then connect the dots

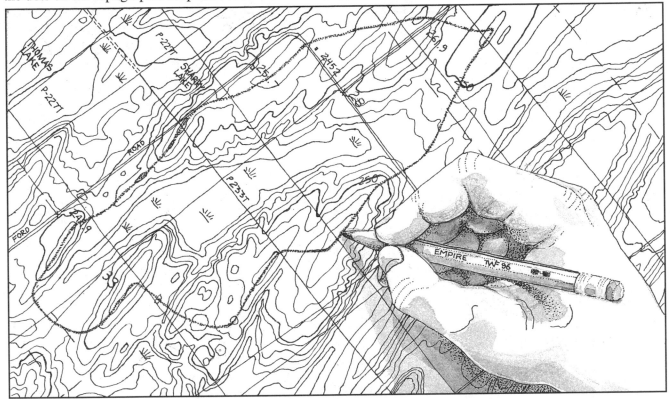

by a line between them that follows the land's high points. This is the boundary of your watershed. (It should be noted that given the scale of even the best topo maps, this process might not work for very small wetlands, as the actual watershed body may not be revealed in the map's resolution.)

To check your watershed mapping, physically tour your wetland's watershed and compare your boundary with identifiable landscape features such as roads, hilltops, lakes, streams, etc. If your wetland's watershed extends beyond your property (as it likely does), remember to ask permission to enter neighboring properties.

Once you have determined what land drains to your wetland, it will be easier for you to recognize what or who may also be affecting your wetland. You may want to continue working with your map, labeling or marking where different activities are occurring, and thinking about the likely effects on your wetland. Essentially, what you are doing is mapping land use and cover type. To do this, consider where current activities that benefit or may harm your wetland are occurring. Where is the intact forest cover? Is there a new subdivision or a plan for one in the watershed? How about shopping malls? What fields are irrigated nearby? Are there animals pastured close to streams or lakes? Are there abandoned fields? Where are manure, fertilizers, or pesticides being spread or sprayed? Have you seen dredging activities in nearby wetlands or water bodies? When you've identified the lands and activities that affect your wetland, then you can start to work with other landowners to cooperatively manage and protect your wetland and the larger ecosystem. An alternative to creating your own maps of the land use and cover type in your watershed may be to acquire a copy of the MIRIS map for your area. Although MIRIS maps are somewhat outdated, they do provide a good snapshot of land use and cover type. However, keep in mind that MIRIS maps were not developed on a watershed basis.

Now, looking beyond the area that directly drains your wetland, use the topo-

graphic map to determine how your wetland is situated in the larger watershed. Depending on the watershed size, you may need to look at several topographic maps. First, determine the streams, rivers, and lakes to which your wetland is connected. Then, using the same procedure used to map the watershed boundary of your wetland, map the watershed boundary of the water bodies to which your wetland is connected. Once this is complete, you can see how your wetland fits into the larger watershed. Alternatively, contact the Surface Water Quality Division of the MDEQ and request a copy of their map of the major watersheds and subwatersheds in Michigan.

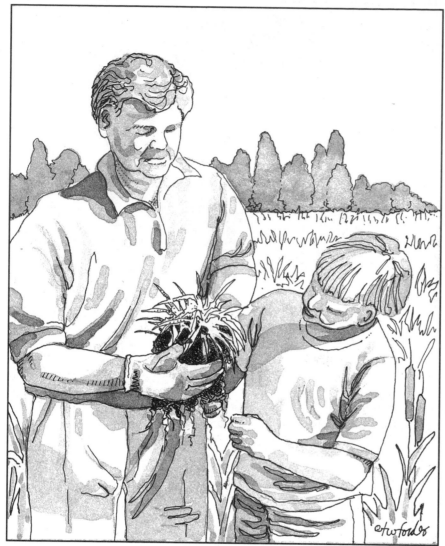

Coupled with a knowledge of surrounding land use, location in the watershed is important when assessing wetland functions such as flood storage, fish and wildlife habitat, and water quality protection. For example, wetlands in the upper reaches of a watershed are generally considered to be more important to flood storage, whereas wetlands directly adjacent to lakes and streams in more developed areas lower in the watershed are generally considered more important to water quality.

You may find that your wetland is not connected to any other surface water. In this case, you may have a bog or other type of isolated wetland. Isolated wetlands provide many important functions, including habitat for rare, threatened, and endangered species, oases for wildlife in developed areas, critical water storage, and in some cases recharge of ground water aquifers. Because many of these functions are dependent upon adjacent land use and proximity to other wetlands and water bodies, it still may be informative to map land use and cover type in the area.

GET YOUR HANDS DIRTY!

By exploring the soils in your wetland, you get a glimpse into the past and can start to understand how the three indicators of wetlands (hydrophytic vegetation, wetland hydrology, and hydric soils) are connected. Soil type is one of the most useful "clues" used to determine whether an area is a wetland. This is because the soils that form under saturated or wet conditions are distinctly different from other soils. A primary difference is the rate at which organic matter (dead plants, leaves, etc.) is decomposed. Both aerobic (requires presence of free oxygen) and anaerobic (does not require free oxygen) bacteria decompose organic matter (mostly carbon compounds). However, decomposition in aerobic conditions happens much more quickly. In upland soils, the spaces between the soil particles are filled with air (which contains plenty of oxygen). Therefore, decomposition is relatively rapid. In saturated soils water replaces the air in the spaces, leaving little or no oxygen available to soil bacteria. As a result, the organic matter decomposes very slowly and accumulates as mucks or peats.

You can observe this by digging a soil pit in your wetland. The soil pit should be large enough to allow you to see several feet down into your wetland. Most wetland soils have an upper layer made up of peat or muck. Muck and peat are composed of the same thing—partially decomposed vegetation. However, the organic matter in mucks has undergone more decomposition than peats. Mucky soils are very dark—sometimes almost black—and feel greasy when rubbed between the fingers. Peats are not as decomposed and usually appear brown in color. When you rub peat between your fingers, you can feel fibers from long-dead vegetation and may be able to make out bits and pieces of moss, grass, wood, and other organic material.

As mentioned in Chapter 3, the soil in your wetland may have a strong odor similar to rotten eggs. In wetland soils that have a mineral component (a layer of clay or sand often located under the layer of peat or muck), you might observe soil color features known as mottling or gleying. Gleyed soils are identified by dull bluish, greenish, or grayish colors. Gleyed soils form when soils are saturated almost all of the time. Mottled soils are identified by a combination of brightly colored splotches of soil in a dull soil matrix. Mottles form due to the movement of ions in the soil column when soils are alternatively saturated and unsaturated during the growing season. Compare these soil characteristics to a soil pit you dig on dry upland ground. Note differences in color, depth of organic material, texture, smell, and wetness. Depending on the amount of iron in your upland soils, it may appear to be a bright reddish-gold color. It is for this reason that many wetland consultants tell their clients to "go for the gold" when determining where to locate houses, roads, and other developments.

EXPLORING HYDROLOGY

Water is the driving force in wetland ecosystems. The presence and duration of water in the soil column and on the surface of the ground influences the soils that form there and the plants that grow there. However, unlike plants that are rooted and relatively easy to identify, and unlike soils that form over thousands of years and can be investigated at any time, wetland hydrology is constantly in flux and difficult to assess.

Ground Water

One way to begin to understand what's happening in regard to your wetland's hydrology is to monitor the water table. You may have already encountered your water table when digging your soil pit. Did you notice any of the indicators of wetland hydrology mentioned in Chapter 3?

Wetland hydrology fluctuates from season to season under the influence of a variety of factors, including rainfall, evapotranspiration from vegetation, temperature, and land use activities in the watershed. The simplest way to measure this fluctuation is to install what is called a piezometer. A piezometer is simply a tube with many small holes or slits in it that is vertically sunk into the ground. Because the slits in the tube let water in, the ground water level in the tube is representative of the ground water level in the soil. On a periodic basis (once every week or so), the water table level is measured, with the measurements being referenced to the surface of the ground. The measurements are then placed on a graph that has the measurements on the vertical axis and the date on the horizontal axis. The resulting line shows the fluctuation in water table depth throughout the year. From this information, you can determine just how long the ground water is influencing the root zone of the wetland.

Surface Water

If your wetland has areas of open water or a stream running through it, a similar procedure can be utilized to measure the fluctuations in the level of the surface water. Instead of a piezometer, you can install what is called a staff gauge. A staff gauge is simply a device to measure surface water fluctuation from a fixed point. A useful staff gauge could simply be a metal rod that is hammered securely into the bottom of the wetland to serve as a reference point (measurements of water levels are made with a separate ruler and based on plus or minus the reference point), or a metal ruler that is attached to a secure post or other immovable object in the water. The location and structure of any staff gauge (if it is intended to be used from year to year) should be selected to withstand projected water flows and the ice that comes with Michigan's winters. As with the piezometer, the staff gauge data can be graphed to show the seasonal fluctuations. In addition, it is also interesting to compare this information with local rainfall data to get an idea of how the water in your wetland is influenced by precipitation and how it may serve as a flood water retention area.

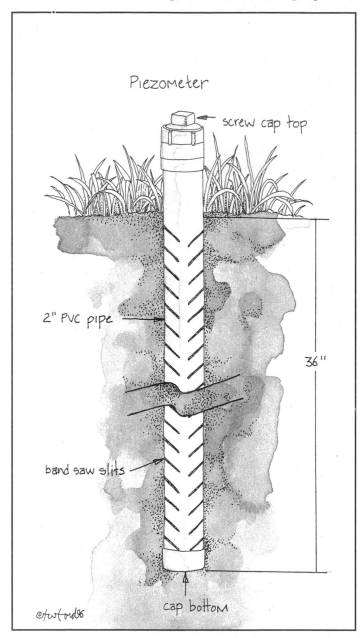

Piezometer

screw cap top

2" PVC pipe

36"

band saw slits

cap bottom

@twtord95

In addition to water levels, if you have a stream entering or leaving your wetland, you may be able to take stream flow (or discharge) measurements to estimate the amount of water coming in and out of your wetland via the stream. The first step in taking stream flow measurements is to measure the stream's velocity. To measure the velocity, you'll need a tape measure or a 50-foot rope length, a highly-visible object that will float freely (an orange works fine), and a stop watch. Pick a section of stream that is not backed up by a dam or debris. Measure 50 feet along the stream bank, drop the orange into the middle of the stream, and record the time it takes for the orange to travel the 50 feet. Do this three times and calculate the average time it takes the orange to travel the distance. Divide the distance (50 feet) by the average time and you will know the approximate speed the water is moving in feet per second. If your stream is moving very slowly, or if you can't find a uniform 50-foot stretch, you might need to reduce the distance. Any timed distance will work adequately. This procedure gives you the surface velocity. The average velocity for the entire column of water is usually a bit slower—approximately 80 percent of the surface velocity.

The next step is to determine how much water is moving at that velocity. To do this, you must first measure the cross-sectional area of the stream. Pick a spot on the stream that is representative of the area where you took the speed measurement. Going across this point perpendicular to the stream flow, measure the total stream width. Next, use a yardstick to measure the depth of the stream at consistent intervals across the stream (one-foot intervals work fine). Average these measurements to give you an average stream depth. The average depth multiplied by the width gives a rough estimate of the cross-sectional area of the stream (in square feet). This value, when multiplied by the speed the stream is flowing (in feet per second) gives you the volume of water that is flowing past that spot (referred to as the stream's discharge) in cubic feet per second (cfs).

If you have a stream flowing through your wetland, try to determine stream flow both upstream and downstream and compare the difference. If you have many

different streams coming into your wetland and only one leaving, you'll have to calculate all incoming streams and add them together before you can compare the quantity of incoming flow to outgoing flow. If the difference is very large, you can assume your wetland is either storing water or releasing water. Try this during different times of the year to see whether there are changes with wet or dry conditions. Some wetlands store water during some parts of the year and release water at others. For many larger streams in Michigan, the United States Geological Survey has recorded stream levels and discharge data. Contact your local government to see if recorded data exists for your stream.

It should be noted that the above activity is not recommended in streams that have mucky bottoms. The reasons for this are twofold: 1) wading in muck in the middle of the stream will stir up sediments, and 2) mucky stream bottoms do not provide sure footing.

PHOTOGRAPHY

With all the wonderful wildlife and plant species available, wetlands are a great place to practice nature photography. Photographs also can be used to document the changes that take place in your wetland as the seasons pass. Select a few different spots within your wetland that represent different habitat types and take pictures at each spot. Return to these same spots through the year and take pictures again. In this way you will have documented the seasonal progression of your wetland.

How serious you are about photographing your wetlands depends on your time, interest, and equipment. A 35mm camera is a minimum requirement. There are hundreds of different lenses from which to choose—practically one for every shot. A macro lens is great for photographing flowers and insects. A telephoto lens can allow you to capture wildlife "up-close and personal." A wide-angle lens is useful for scenic landscape shots. Your choice of film should be geared to your available light (considering shade, time of day, time of year, cloud conditions, etc.), potential use of the photos (e.g., snapshots for the family album or color slides for a civic club presentation), and most importantly personal preference. Wildlife and nature

photography is a challenging art. If you aspire to learn more about this art form, consider taking a course at your community college or arts center.

A wetland naturally changes in character as the years go by. If you make a point to take pictures from the same spot—say every five years—you may eventually be able to see the subtle changes that are occurring in your wetland as it ages. Change should occur gradually over a long period of time. A noticeable difference from year to year in vegetation communities, ground water levels, or newly eroded banks may indicate that the integrity of the wetland is being adversely affected, and suggests the need for land use management and protection efforts.

SUMMARY

The information included in this chapter provides an overview of the ways in which a landowner can explore his or her wetland. Many of these activities are more enjoyable when shared with other family members. Like a good friend, as you learn more about your wetland you will better understand and appreciate its unique character. In addition, you will have a better understanding of how your wetland functions and how it is influenced by other land uses in the watershed. With this information, you will be able to better determine appropriate management options, have a basis of ecological understanding to help you work with other landowners in your area, and understand the work of consultants and land use managers hired to provide you with wetland services.

Developing a Conservation Management Strategy

Just as wetlands support diversity of plant and animal life, there are a diversity of issues involved with developing and implementing a wetland conservation management plan. Landowners vary by life style, financial circumstances, and conservation goals. Wetlands vary by type, size, location in the state, surrounding land use patterns, functions, and values. Management options range from "do nothing" to active manipulation of water and vegetation to enhance certain functions. And the range of protection options and landowner wetland programs is equally broad. Considering all these options, there is the potential for literally hundreds of thousands of different landowner wetland conservation management plans. It is obvious that no one cookbook method or process will meet the needs of every landowner. This chapter provides a framework that helps you consider all the influencing factors and management options.

BACKGROUND FACTORS

There are a number of background factors critical to the development of any sort of management plan. These factors help you to define your goals and objectives, evaluate the property, and assess problems and opportunities. The range of factors that must be acknowledged and considered can be divided into two broad categories: the unique circumstances of the individual and the unique nature of the land. With adequate consideration of these factors, the most suitable conservation management strategy can be developed.

The Unique Circumstances of the Individual

Paramount among the background factors to consider are your own interests, needs, and desires. Each wetland property owner owns their land for unique reasons. Some have specifically sought to purchase wetlands for the solitude and passive recreation opportunities they provide. Others own wetlands that are inci-

dental to their main interest in the property. And yet others have property that contains wetlands that have been passed down for generations—either in the form of a cottage for summer recreation, hunting land, or agricultural land for business purposes. This chapter assumes that regardless of how you came to own your wetland, you have some interest in protecting it. The manner in which you protect your land depends on a variety of individual circumstances, including:

1) Age and personal health;
2) Whether you live on the property;
3) Your desired use of the property;
4) The interests of your children in the property;
5) Whether your major financial assets are associated with the property containing the wetland;
6) Whether your income needs are met by current or expected income;
7) The extent to which the financial carrying costs of continuing to own the land (i.e., taxes, miscellaneous maintenance, etc.) are affordable; and,
8) How your personal financial situation will influence tax benefits of various land protection strategies.

When looking at the range of individual life style, income, investment, and conservation interest circumstances, it becomes clear that each landowner is in a unique situation in regard to the best strategy to protect their wetlands. Acknowledging these unique circumstances will help you determine what path is best for you. You may find that you have several objectives which either cannot be achieved entirely or which may not be compatible with each other.

The Unique Nature of the Land

Just as the circumstances of every landowner are unique, so too is every wetland. As you have seen elsewhere in this guidebook, wetlands are extremely diverse. Their functions and values are influenced by everything from their own physical characteristics (soil, vegetation, hydrology, size, etc.) to present and past surrounding land use patterns. Accordingly, the management needs and opportunities provided by the wetland also vary widely. The task of restoring a former wetland to its original state may require intensive effort that includes research about what it was like originally, careful design and implementation of restoration plans, ongoing maintenance to ensure that the desired plant and animal species are becoming established, and long-term monitoring to ensure that the project was successful. On the other hand, a fully functioning wetland in a watershed that had not undergone environmental degradation is better managed by a do-nothing approach with a thoughtful eye toward external activities in the surrounding area that could threaten it. To be successful, the management plan for your wetland and the method that you use to protect it must respect the opportunities and constraints as determined by the unique nature of your wetland.

TOWARDS DEVELOPING A CONSERVATION MANAGEMENT STRATEGY

As noted above, given the range of unique individual circumstances and the range of wetlands in Michigan, it is difficult to develop a comprehensive conservation strategy process that will work for everyone. Chapter 6 provides a "decision tree" to help you determine which method of permanent protection is best for you. Chapter 8 provides a process that can be used when considering activities to restore, enhance, and create wetlands. The purpose of this chapter is to provide you with a series of items that must be considered and questions that must be answered to help you develop your own conservation management strategy.

Establish Goals and Objectives

The first step in developing a conservation management plan is to establish goals and objectives. To be most effective, your goals must be compatible with the conditions of the wetland and surrounding properties, and acknowledge your individual circumstances. As you go through a management planning process, you uncover more information about your wetland. Accordingly, it is important to keep in mind that your goals may need to be changed in light of new information. Below are several questions to be answered that will help shape your conservation management goals.

1) What sort of wetland-based recreational activities do you enjoy?
2) What ecological functions do you most want your wetland to provide?
3) Are the answers to questions one and two compatible with the size, type, location, and surrounding uses of your wetland?
4) What is your need for income from your property and its wetlands?

5) What is your ability to carry costs of owning and managing the property and its wetlands?
6) What are your estate planning interests?
7) What is your family's interest in retaining or living on the property?
8) Do you want to leave a legacy of permanent wetland protection?
9) Are there other special needs to be considered?

Evaluate the Specific Property

The exploration activities in Chapter 4 will help you evaluate the specific property. If you are most interested in wetland restoration or enhancement, the information in Chapter 8 will be useful. Depending on how involved you plan on getting, there will be a point at which you will need to consult with wetland experts to help develop your conservation management strategy. Here are some questions that will assist you in evaluating the wetlands on your property.

1) What are the physical characteristics of your wetland? (size, hydrology, soils, vegetation, etc.)
2) What functions and values does the wetland provide?
3) Have there been any changes to the wetland's characteristics that have impacted the wetland's functions? (drainage, filling, vegetation clearing, etc.)
4) Do you own the entire wetland, or are there other property owners who could impact the wetland?
5) What is the condition of the upland surrounding the wetland?
6) Can the upland part of the property be developed without damaging the wetlands? (e.g., is there enough space to establish and maintain adequate buffers between the wetland and building sites or access roads)
7) How compatible is the existing wetland with your goals for the property?
8) Does any of the information generated by the above questions suggest that the overall goals that you have developed for the management strategy need to be changed?

Evaluate the Surrounding Lands

As noted throughout this guidebook, what happens on the land around your wetland impacts what happens in your wetland. When considering management strategies, it is important to be aware of the external factors affecting your wetland that might impact meeting your goals.

1) What are the land use trends and associated land use change inducers? (e.g., roads, sewers, etc.)
2) What are the land ownership patterns and interests of neighboring landowners?
3) What are the current zoning and other land use controls?
4) What are the real estate market conditions? (as indicated by current listings and recent comparable sales)
5) What are the characteristics of the area's natural landscapes and watershed, and their suitability for conservation and development?
6) Does any of the information generated by the above questions suggest that the overall goals for the management strategy need to be changed?

Assess Problems and Opportunities

The information gathered by answering the questions above will have identified problems and opportunities in regard to accomplishing your goals given your wetland and your personal financial situation. The points to consider below help to organize those problems and opportunities.

1) Physical Considerations: What are the problems and opportunities provided by the physical characteristics of the wetland, the upland that you control, and the watershed that directly influences it? The physical considerations will determine what active management activities will be beneficial and if restoration, enhancement, or creation activities will be successful.
2) Legal Considerations: What (if any) are the limitations placed upon the property or its wetlands by existing federal or state regulations, deed restrictions, and/or municipal zoning? These limitations may involve securing a permit for intended activities.
3) Market Considerations: What is the property's potential use based upon local real estate market trends and the property's physical characteristics? How will the proposed activities impact the market value of your property?
4) Financial Considerations: What are the likely current and future costs and income related to maintaining the wetlands on the property, considering the current condition and implementation of any management and protection strategy? What are the human, financial, technical, and material resources available to you?
5) Goals: How do these considerations influence your goals for the wetland and your property as a whole? Can your original goals be met, or do they need to be modified?

Develop Alternatives

Based on the above considerations, it's time to start putting together alternatives. The following chapters provide basic information regarding methods of permanent protection available to the landowner; management activities to protect wetlands; and a process for wetland restoration, creation, and enhancement. If your potential activities involve dredging, filling, draining, or construction in a wetland, permits may be needed. Chapter 9 contains a discussion of state and federal wet-

land regulatory requirements. The final chapter provides information on where to go for more help, including state and federal landowner assistance programs, nongovernmental programs, and how to select a consultant. When putting together the package for your conservation strategy, be creative and utilize various options. For example, whether you take a hands-off approach and let your intact well-functioning wetland do its own thing, or you restore a formerly drained wetland, you can protect it in perpetuity with a conservation easement granted to a qualified organization. Depending on the nature of your plan, it may be necessary to consult with professionals in a range of fields to help you develop reasonable alternatives. If you have not involved individuals and organizations who might play a role in implementing elements of your strategy, it is especially important to involve them at this stage.

Select Alternatives

Once you have developed alternatives, it's time to select the one that best meets your goals, benefits the environment, and is within your financial means. When it comes to making this decision, the importance of consulting with environmental and conservation organizations or wetland consultants, tax lawyers and other financial advisors, and agency staff who administer landowner incentive programs cannot be overemphasized.

Implement the Plan

Again, the tasks associated with implementing your plan will depend upon the plan. One of the key elements to successfully implementing any conservation strategy is coordinating the work of individuals and organizations who are critical to accomplishing plan components. If you have identified the constraints, opportunities, and available resources effectively; set your goals realistically and with respect to the ecosystem; and coordinated all the involved individuals and organizations, you will be successful.

Voluntary Protection Options

Because of their love for the land, many property owners want to permanently protect their wetlands. Donations or sale of property to a conservation organization, or the creation of what is known as a conservation easement, can effectively protect wetlands in perpetuity, allowing landowners to pass on a legacy of bountiful natural resources to their children and grandchildren. In addition to benefiting your family, society benefits from the voluntary and permanent protection of wetlands. Because of this, provisions in the tax codes allow for financial benefits in the form of income and property tax reductions. Wetland regulations exempt many activities that impact wetlands. Voluntary protection options can serve to protect wetlands to a greater extent than regulations. This chapter describes the primary methods of voluntary wetland protection.

PERMANENT PROTECTION OPTIONS

The methods of voluntary wetland protection can be divided into two categories: those that offer permanent protection and those that serve as nonbinding protection agreements. Permanent protection options serve to ensure that your management goals for your wetland will be met in perpetuity.

Donation

Donation of land has long played an important role in the protection of natural areas. It continues to be important because of its effectiveness, its relative simplicity, and its financial benefits to the landowner. By execution of a deed, the owner gives his or her land (or a specified part of it) for conservation purposes to a qualified nonprofit organization or governmental agency. A donor's gift of land is tax deductible. Each donation of land has different tax advantages for different individuals. Different types of taxes (e.g., real property taxes, gift taxes, estate taxes, or income taxes) are affected differently in each situation. Landowners

considering donation of wetland property are encouraged to retain a tax attorney or accountant to analyze the tax consequences of his or her particular situation.

There are several variations on the donation theme: outright donation, bargain sale, donation with a reserved life estate, and a bequest. With a bargain sale, the land is conveyed at a price below fair market value, which may be attractive to a landowner who can not afford to convey the land without some compensation. A bargain sale is part gift and part sale. The sale price is determined jointly by the landowner and the recipient. For federal income tax purposes, it can result in both a taxable sale and a charitable contribution deduction, depending on the particular circumstances.

Erie Marsh Preserve

The Erie Shooting and Fishing Club was established in the 1870's to capitalize on the natural abundance of the Lake Erie marshes near the town of Erie, just north of Toledo.

Over time, and under the name of the Ottawa Bay Development Company, this group of concerned sportsmen assembled 2,168 acres of woods and wetlands, including some of the most productive marshes in all of southeast Michigan.

Recognizing the ecological significance of the marshes and their importance to all kinds of waterfowl, the Club turned to The Nature Conservancy in 1978. They donated the entire tract of land to the Conservancy to be used and maintained as a Conservancy preserve. The Conservancy recognized that duck hunting would not jeopardize the wetland characteristics of the marsh, and the Club, interested in continuing their long-standing tradition of duck hunting in the marsh, received a license to continue duck hunting on approximately one-half of the property. The Club continues to maintain the property, at Club expense, and pays a fee for the license agreement and right to use the property during hunting season. At all other times of the year, the property is open to the public for bird watching, hiking, and nature photography.

Out of this creative agreement, the Club received the right to continue to hunt the property during duck hunting season; received a tax deduction for the value of the gift of land donated to The Nature Conservancy; and was secure in the knowledge that the property would continue to be maintained as a nature sanctuary. The Nature Conservancy received a gift of 2,168 acres of productive marshland, and now owns and manages one of the best birding sites in the lower Great Lakes.

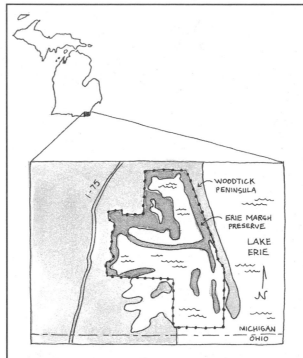

A donation with a reserved life estate is a donation in which the donor retains possession and use of the property for his or her lifetime. An income tax deduction is allowed for the value of a charitable contribution, which is the difference between the property's fair market value and its value under the provisions of the donation with a reserved life estate. The Internal Revenue Service takes into account the number of years that a donor with a reserved life estate is likely to enjoy the use of the property. Thus, such a donation will yield greater tax benefits to an older donor.

A bequest is a donation of land in an owner's will. Although such a donation does not enable the donor to realize an income tax deduction, the value of the bequest is deductible in determining the donor's taxable estate, which can benefit heirs by reducing estate taxes.

Donation of natural land has a number of potential income and estate tax advantages. Such donation may also significantly reduce the costs of land ownership, such as real estate taxes. However, the extent of those financial benefits will depend upon the kind of donation, the donor's particular financial situation, and prevailing federal tax law at the time the donation occurs. The major incentive for donation of natural land is that it offers the most simple and effective tool available to the landowner who wants to protect his or her wetland. When contemplating donating your land to a nonprofit organization or a governmental entity, it is important to have a solid understanding of how the recipient organization will manage the property. You should find out how the organization might manage the property and make sure that the potential uses correspond to your desires. If the organization wants to reserve the right to sell the property in the future, you may want to consider granting a conservation easement to a third party to ensure that the land will be protected by future owners.

Conservation Easements

A conservation easement is a voluntary agreement that is used to transfer certain rights concerning the use of land to a qualified nonprofit organization, governmental body, or other legal entity without transferring title to the land. In Michigan, Part 21 of the Michigan Natural Resources and Environmental Code (Act 451 of 1994) (formerly the Conservation and Historic Preservation Easement Act; Public Act 197 of 1980), authorizes the creation of voluntary conservation easements. A conservation easement under this statute can provide limitations on

Lake Bellaire Wetland Easement

A conservation easement is a very flexible tool which allows a landowner to protect the natural resource values of their property while maintaining ownership. The size of the property under easement and the limitations placed on the property can all vary depending on the wishes of the landowner, the goals of the conservation organization, and the statutory guidelines.

There are hundreds of conservation easements in Michigan which protect wetland and other valuable habitats. Thanks to Marilyn Fisher and her family, 89 acres of forest, the majority of which is wetland, along 4,000 feet of shoreline on Lake Bellaire in Antrim County will forever be protected under a conservation easement signed with the Grand Traverse Regional Land Conservancy. The conservation easement allows selective harvesting of cedar for the family's use on their property adjacent to the easement and recreational uses such as hunting, fishing, and hiking.

The wetland protected by Mrs. Fisher's conservation easement has long been a concern of the Michigan Loon Preservation Society and the Three Lakes Association. The Common Loon, a threatened species in Michigan, uses the wetland for nesting and safety cover. The large forested wetland system on the property serves as a filtration system for nutrients and sediments that otherwise would enter Lake Bellaire and potentially lead to long-term water quality problems if degraded.

Mrs. Fisher is a former member of the Board of Trustees of the Grass River Natural Area and has had a keen interest in land and water conservation for many years. Establishing the conservation easement was a way for Mrs. Fisher to take an active role in protecting the natural resources of her community. "These lakes are very special and we can't afford to take them for granted," said Fisher.

the use of, or can prohibit certain acts on, a parcel of land. The easement is considered a conveyance of real property and must be recorded with the registrar of deeds in the appropriate county to be enforceable against a subsequent purchaser of the property.

Conservation easements are flexible, effective, and allow the landowner to maintain ownership of the property. A common misconception about conservation easements is that the land must be open to public access. The public does not have access to property protected by a conservation easement unless the landowner who grants the easement specifically allows it. Conservation easements may be drafted to meet particular circumstances and objectives of an individual landowner. They can allow for uses compatible with wetland protection (e.g., nature study and passive outdoor recreation such as walking). They can identify areas on a property

that will be reserved for future development. They can protect the easement area against disturbances that are not covered by wetland regulations, such as vegetation clearing. In short, conservation easements are a powerful tool that enable you to manage your land in a particular way well into the future.

To be eligible for a tax deduction, conservation easements must be granted in perpetuity by the landowner. Several tax benefits may be available to the grantor, including deduction of the value of an easement as a charitable contribution, as determined by the amount by which the easement reduces the market value of the property. The Internal Revenue Code normally allows an itemized deduction of up to 30 percent of an individual's adjusted gross income for such contributions. Amounts in excess of the 30 percent limitation may be carried over and deducted during the next five years (this applies to donations of land also). The easement may reduce the value of the property if it is included in the individual's taxable estate. In addition, the development restrictions placed on a property by a conservation easement may also result in reducing property taxes. As with land donations, if you are considering granting a conservation easement, you should contact an attorney or accountant for an analysis of possible tax benefits based on your financial situation.

Deed Restrictions and Covenants

Deed restrictions are clauses placed in deeds restricting the future use of land. When property containing wetlands is transferred, deed restrictions can prohibit uses or activities by the new owners that would destroy, damage, or modify wetlands. A covenant is a contract between a landowner and another party stating that the landowner will use, or refrain from using, their land in a certain manner. Like a deed restriction, a covenant can require that landowners refrain from activities that will damage wetlands. Once placed in deeds, covenants become deed restrictions.

Mutual covenants involve agreements between nearby or adjacent landowners to control the future use of their land through restrictions agreed upon by all participating landowners. The fact that multiple landowners participate in the covenant provides greater incentive to comply with the terms of the covenant. However, getting numerous property owners to voluntarily agree on certain management practices can be very challenging.

Although deed restrictions and covenants have been used across the country to protect wetlands, their use in Michigan is not as effective as conservation easements. This is primarily for two reasons. First, unlike a conservation easement that is granted to and signed by an organization that has a commitment and responsibility to resource protection, the enforcement of deed restrictions and covenants is less reliable. Because deed restrictions are placed in the deed and run with the land, there is no continuity of oversight, unlike the continuous ownership of an easement holder. Hence, with a deed restriction, you're relying on the concern and commitment of some unidentified body to provide the oversight. Second, it is relatively easy for a future landowner to petition the courts to vacate a particular deed restriction. Although it is theoretically possible to modify a conservation easement, many changes are prohibited by federal regulations where income tax deductions are involved and all signatories to the easement must agree to proposed changes. It is unlikely that a qualified organization would agree to modifications of a conservation easement that would result in adverse wetland impacts. Another major difference between conservation easements and deed restrictions or covenants is that the loss in market value due to deed restrictions and covenants cannot be claimed as a charitable deduction on income tax returns.

Sale

Sometimes a landowner is in a situation where they must sell their wetland for financial or other reasons. In regard to protecting wetlands, the values and land use interests of the person who purchases the wetland are of paramount concern. If you must sell your wetland, but are concerned about its future protection, you can consider using some of the tools above to permanently restrict activities that degrade wetlands before you sell. For example, one of the beauties of a conservation easement is that it runs with the title in perpetuity. Prior to listing the property for sale, the wetland portion of the property may be protected by a conservation easement granted to a local conservancy or other qualified entity. The bargain sale option provides substantial tax benefits to the seller while reducing the purchase price for the buyer.

Another way to help ensure protection of your wetland after it is sold is to seek a purchaser who shares your values and goals regarding wetland protection and property management. If the area provides wildlife habitat, then advertising its availability in hunting magazines will get you in touch with individuals who may want to manage it for hunting purposes. Don't limit your search for a buyer to individuals. Nonprofit organizations such as The Nature Conservancy, local land conservancies, Michigan Audubon Society, and many others own property and may be interested in yours. In addition, local units of government may be interested in your property for the purpose of preserving community open space and passive recreation areas. Contact these organizations and entities to gauge their interest in purchasing your property. Don't be discouraged if your offer to sell them your wetland is not immediately accepted. These entities have limited budgets for property acquisition and most have fairly specific guidelines that must be met before they can justify purchasing a parcel. Another option is to sell your property to your local unit of government. The Michigan Natural Resources Trust Fund provides grants to local units to assist in purchase of significant natural lands.

If you identify a willing organization or agency that you would like to see purchase your property in the future, you may consider granting a right of first refusal to that organization. A right of first refusal binds you to giving the conservation organization or agency the option to match the purchase offer and acquire the land if you are approached by another buyer. This gives the conservation organization extra time to acquire funds necessary to purchase the land.

Another way to generate income from the wetland is to rent or lease the land to a conservation or hunting organization for a specified purpose and period of time. Certain restrictions can be incorporated into the lease to guide the activities of the lessee, including provisions to terminate the lease if the property is not used in an appropriate manner.

Designing Development to Protect Wetlands

For those landowners who desire to develop their property for residential and commercial use, wetland protection can be integrated into your development plan. In many cases across Michigan, residential lots adjacent to a protected wetland fetched higher sale prices than nearby lots not adjacent to the wetland.

To plan development to protect wetlands, you must first conduct an assessment of the wetland that would include (at a minimum): wetland boundaries, wetland size, wetland type, connections to other bodies of water, and critical upland habitat that should be protected along with the wetland. Once this is determined, the next step is to determine what type of development is compatible with protecting the wetlands on the site while still meeting your financial desires. The layout for the buildings and roads should be designed in a way that avoids wetlands and minimizes wetland crossings as much as possible. How the upland adjacent to a wetland will be developed has important implications for the long-term health of the wetland. Important considerations include the establishment of greenbelts and buffer zones around wetlands, managing the quantity and quality of the stormwater that will be generated in a way that does not harm the wetland, human access and use of

Uplands of Scio Ridge

Wetlands in residential environments can serve as important visual and recreational amenities, function as stormwater storage and cleansing systems, and provide spatial definition of the landscape. In Southeast Michigan, an area dominated by agricultural and built environments, wetlands are frequently the only "natural" features remaining on properties to be developed or redeveloped with housing.

Courtesy of Johnson, Johnson, and Roy, Inc.

In the case of one development, the Uplands of Scio Ridge located just west of Ann Arbor, wetlands serve as a natural structure that organizes and defines neighborhoods. Wetland areas and drainage corridors are also planned to be incorporated in future phases of the project as the focus of passive recreational activity. Trails, boardwalks, and observation platforms will provide access along the wetland perimeter, and in selected locations, into the interior of the wetland. Preservation of the wetlands and drainage corridors, buffer zones, and the adjacent upland forest provides a rural character for the site and protects the ability of these systems to function naturally.

As more detailed planning and engineering studies are prepared for this project, methods can be investigated to further protect the wetlands. These include approaches such as native landscaping in community open spaces, managing stormwater with grassed swales rather than pipes, use of stormwater infiltration basins to recharge the ground water, and restoring wetland and stream areas previously impacted by agricultural activities. Protecting the integrity of the natural systems enhances the values of these features and those of the residential development as a living environment.

the wetland, and land use practices (e.g., fertilizer and pesticide use) that will be in place once the property is fully developed.

After a plan for the property has been developed that will protect the wetland over time, you have many options to help put that plan into place. Implementing the protection measures through a conservation easement can result in substantial tax benefits. Likewise, donating the portion of the property that is to be protected to a qualified organization will result in tax benefits. Ensuring that upland practices such as lawn maintenance are compatible with wetland protection often provide the largest challenge when attempting to design developments to protect wetlands. The best way to do this depends on the pattern of ownership in the development. With a condominium-type ownership pattern, the developer retains responsibility to manage the property. However, in a traditional subdivision ownership pattern, unacceptable land use practices may need to be prohibited through deed restrictions or covenants. A neighborhood or property owner's association can serve to enforce the deed restrictions.

This is a very brief sketch of what's involved when a property owner desires to integrate wetland protection into a development. If you plan to take this course, it is highly recommended that you hire a reputable consultant who is knowledgeable about wetland ecology, wetland law, land use planning, and local planning and zoning requirements. Some helpful hints on how to select a consultant who will best meet your needs are included in Chapter 10.

VOLUNTARY NONBINDING PROGRAMS

The tools listed above provide landowners with mechanisms to protect wetlands for the long term. However, some landowners are not comfortable with committing to permanent protection of their property. For these individuals, there are several approaches that encourage wetland protection in a nonbinding and nonregulatory manner. These programs provide technical assistance and show that there is public support for landowner wetland protection activities.

Michigan Natural Areas Registry

The Michigan Chapter of The Nature Conservancy promotes

The Nature Conservancy's Registry Program

In 1995, Bruce and Raven Wallace approached The Nature Conservancy because they had recently bought a beautiful and wild piece of coast within the project boundary of the Northern Lake Huron Bioreserve in the Upper Peninsula. With 400 acres and over a mile of shoreline, they wanted to explore ways to protect their property and the bay that surrounds them.

Bruce is an attorney in Ann Arbor and has always been supportive of conservation. Raven is a computer scientist at University of Michigan, and together they are kept busy raising three children. Their property is nestled in the foot of a 2,500 acre bay and is dotted by marshes, a small island, beaver dams, cedar swamps, and an inland lake and bog. It adjoins the National Forest to the west and a preserve owned by the Little Traverse Conservancy to the east. They recently built a small cabin back from the shoreline, but theirs is the only cabin on the bay.

THE NORTHERN LAKE HURON BIORESERVE

The Wallaces wanted to protect the unique habitat of the bay and the species that use it. They have healthy populations of Hughton's goldenrod, a federally threatened plant, along the bay's outer shoreline. Loons nest on the inland lake and feed in the bay waters. Bruce has watched Bald Eagles fishing from the trees around their home and the calls of peepers, wood frogs, chorus frogs, tree frogs and toads are so loud on spring nights that it is hard to sleep.

Because they still have many years of work and parenting ahead of them, the best protection option for them is the Registry program. They receive information about their property from the Conservancy and in turn agree to protect those values to the best of their ability. If they ever decide to sell their property, they agree to contact the Conservancy. The Conservancy, in turn, calls them once or twice a year to say hello, answer any questions, and pass on any new information they have about the area.

The Registry is a voluntary agreement. Until a time when the Wallaces may be willing and able to consider a donation of a conservation easement or possibly even a gift of land, the Registry is a great way for the Wallaces and the Conservancy to keep in touch and ensure that, through the efforts of the private landowner, an important part of Michigan's landscape is protected for future generations.

the preservation of important natural areas, including wetlands, through voluntary nonregulatory agreements between landowners and The Nature Conservancy. The Michigan Natural Features Inventory (MNFI), a program partially supported by funds from The Nature Conservancy, provides a listing of significant natural areas in the state. The Nature Conservancy staff provides outreach to the landowners of significant areas to develop positive relationships and voluntary protection agreements. To qualify for the Registry, a property must be either ecologically significant, such as an unusual wetland or old growth forest, or be a relict plant community (survivors from climates and ecosystems of the past), or be habitat for rare, threatened, or endangered plants or animals. If you think you have wetlands that qualify, contact The Nature Conservancy for information on how you can nominate your land to be entered in their Michigan Natural Areas Registry.

Natural Heritage Stewardship Program

Coordinated by the Michigan Natural Features Inventory, this program promotes the voluntary preservation of endangered or threatened species and their habitats. Currently, the program focuses on threatened species that inhabit the Great Lakes shoreline and interdunal swale wetlands, including Houghton's goldenrod, dwarf lake iris, Piping Plover, and Pitcher's thistle. The program uses information from the MNFI to target properties which may have significant habitat. The pur-

pose of the project is to contact landowners and provide information regarding how to protect and enhance significant habitat areas either on their property or on nearby state land. Landowners who participate in voluntary stewardship activities receive a certificate of recognition and a limited edition wildlife print. Since wetlands are the home for more endangered and threatened species than any other landform, this program helps to raise awareness and encourage proper stewardship of wetlands.

Wetland Stewardship Programs

Many local organizations coordinate wetland stewardship programs. For example, in northern lower Michigan, the Tip of the Mitt Watershed Council has developed a Wetland Stewardship Program to involve landowners in wetland protection who may not be ready to commit to permanent protection. The Watershed Council has identified wetland owners in their service area and encouraged them to become wetland stewards. The goal of the program is to protect wetlands through voluntary commitments from the owners of the resource.

The Wetland Stewardship Program promotes the protection of wetlands through voluntary, nonbinding agreements between wetland owners and the Watershed Council. The wetland steward agrees not to drain, dredge, fill, or in any other way destroy his or her wetland. They also agree to notify the Watershed Council when they plan to sell the land or if they decide not to participate any longer in the Stewardship Program. In return for becoming a Wetland Steward, the Watershed Council provides assistance regarding land management, advice on other protection measures, and a certificate of appreciation. Hopefully, the wetland stewards also receive the satisfaction and pride which come from knowing they have helped protect Michigan's wetlands. If you are interested in this sort of program, contact the conservation organizations that serve your area. If they do not currently have such a program, help them develop one!

WHAT'S RIGHT FOR ME?

The options listed above can be used individually or in combination. The decision as to what options are right for you depend on a variety of factors that were introduced in the last chapter. For the purposes of this chapter, the best options can be determined by answering four questions:

1) Do you want to continue to own your wetland?
2) Do you want to manage the property exclusively?
3) Do you want compensation for selling the property?
4) Do you want to restrict future use of the wetland when property title is transferred?

Landowner Protection Decision Tree

Do you want to continue to own your wetland?

Yes   No

Do you want to manage the property exclusively?

Yes	No
• Voluntary Nonbinding Stewardship Agreements.	• Conservation Easements • Lease • Deed Restrictions • Mutual Covenants • Transfer of Development Rights

Do you want compensation for selling the property?

Yes	No

• Sale:
  • Full Market
  • Bargain
  • Right of First Refusal
	• Donation:
	  • Outright
	  • Bequest w/Reserved Life Estate

Do you want to voluntarily restrict future use of the wetland when property title is transferred (upon death)?

Yes	No
• Conservation Easement (prior to transfer)	• Normal Title Transfer

Do you want to voluntarily restrict future use of the wetland when property title is transferred?

Yes	No
• Conservation Easement (prior to transfer)	• Normal Title Transfer

---

The decision tree above provides a step-through process incorporating these questions. It is important to note that any transaction (conservation easement, sale, or bargain sale) involving a land conservancy or governmental body must be arranged in advance with the appropriate representatives to be sure that the project is acceptable to the organization or agency. Land conservancies, other conservation organizations, and agencies each have their own criteria regarding accepting conservation easements or acquiring properties. It would be very frustrating for you to make decisions, hire attorneys and tax advisors, etc. based on an assumption that the organization or agency would be interested, only to find out that your project does not meet their specific criteria.

Voluntary protection efforts have grown substantially in Michigan over the last decade. The growth in the number of donations, conservation easements, and

wetland purchases by conservation organizations and agencies has been phenomenal. Although income and property tax reductions have served as an incentive, the greater driving force is the heart of the landowner. Landowners who voluntarily protect their land beyond what is required by regulation do it because they want to preserve their property in its natural state for the long term. Their sense of stewardship is so strong that they want the property to be cared for long after they are gone. This commitment is exemplary and will serve as a model for others who care about preserving the opportunities of future generations to enjoy the benefits of wetlands.

Management to Protect Your Wetland

The most important thing to remember about managing to protect your wetland is to work with what you have. Chapter 4 provides some activities to help you explore your wetland and better understand the physical characteristics, functions, and values that it provides. For many wetland property owners, the best way to manage the wetland for protection and maintenance of the functions it serves is a hands-off approach. The hands-off approach means that you are not actively changing the key components of the wetland to modify the functions it naturally provides. It means that you are conscious of the potential threats to your wetland and are actively managing those threats. If you can protect a wetland and its surrounding uplands from potential threats, the wetland will take care of itself and provide a range of beneficial functions. This chapter briefly describes some of the activities which impact wetlands and alter the functions they provide. In addition, some management practices are discussed to help protect your wetland.

ACTIVITIES WHICH IMPACT WETLAND FUNCTIONS

Assuming that your wetland has not undergone changes such as dredging, filling, topsoil removal, draining, or other major changes that would severely alter its type and function (in other words, "normal" conditions exist), your wetland is in the location and of the type best suited for the unique hydrologic, climatic, subsurface geologic, and soil conditions found on your property. Accordingly, it is providing valuable functions that contribute to the health and well-being of the surrounding landscape. Below is a list of activities which impact the natural functions of intact wetlands. Some of these activities, such as dredging, filling, draining, and construction in wetlands, are regulated. Others, such as vegetation removal or the natural invasion by exotic species are not. For a more complete discussion of wetland regulations, see Chapter 9.

Hydrologic Modifications

Water is the lifeblood of wetland ecosystems. Just as maintaining natural hydrology of a wetland is the key to protecting it, activities that alter hydrology of a wetland can severely degrade it. Even small changes in hydrology, like changing the amount of surface water entering and leaving a wetland or changing the ground water table a few inches either up or down, can have dramatic impacts on the way a wetland functions, including how much flood protection a wetland provides, how much sediment and pollutants it can remove from surface water, what sort of vegetation can live there, what wildlife habitat it provides, and how the wetland relates to other bodies of water. Ironically, many of these activities are done with the intention of improving wetlands. A few specific activities that influence wetland hydrology are addressed below.

Flooding

Impounding water behind a dam or conveying additional water to a wetland results in the raising of surface and ground water levels. Such projects are often undertaken to create wildlife floodings. Although floodings have created additional wetland wildlife habitat in former uplands, they have also resulted in changes to the original wetlands that existed in the area that was flooded. The results of an analysis of the habitat benefits of flooding projects can depend on the perspective of the person making the assessment. Regardless of who is making the assessment, it is clear that either impounding water or otherwise increasing the water that enters a wetland can cause changes in the vegetation community, the animals that live there, water quality maintenance functions, and flood storage and conveyance.

Not all flooding is caused by human-induced factors. Beaver dams are one of nature's ways of creating a wetland, but also of flooding existing wetlands. As with human-induced impoundments, beaver dams can change wetland systems. In Michigan, the typical notion about beaver dams is that they should be removed. However, in areas where beavers have long been a part of the landscape and wetland vegetation communities have formed in response to long-term beaver activity, their activities provide a beneficial service to many other species. Mink, raccoons, and green-backed herons utilize beaver-created wetlands when hunting for frogs, crayfish, and other prey. The beaver lodge and dam serve as good basking areas for snakes and turtles, and frogs and salamanders breed in the shallow waters that are created. The dead trees that result from beaver floodings harbor insects that are fed upon by woodpeckers. The holes made by woodpeckers in turn provide habitat for cavity nesting birds such as the wood duck and hooded merganser. In other areas, however, where new beaver dams will impact water quality (primarily the warming of trout streams), change vegetation communities in an undesired way, or adversely impact roads or houses, they are typically considered negative (see Beaver Management below).

Draining

The flip-side of flooding a wetland is draining it. The United States has a long history of draining wetlands. Since the early years of this country, there have been governmental programs to fund the draining of wetlands. In fact, the Michigan Drain Code still provides a mechanism to tax landowners in a watershed to pay for drainage activities, many of which impact wetlands.

Activities which result in draining wetlands include ditch construction, the laying of field tiles (subsurface pipes with holes that collect water from the soil and convey it to a lower point), and the removal or alteration of structures that impound water (beaver dams, roads, etc.). Drainage has many adverse effects on wetlands and the surrounding watershed. The wetland itself undergoes dramatic vegetation changes as less water-tolerant species colonize the area. As a result, wetland dependent insect, amphibian, reptile, bird, and mammal species are lost and other animals suited to uplands take their place. Drainage also severely impacts water quality. Instead of the wetland trapping sediment and nutrients, thus protecting the receiving waters from pollutants, the soils in the wetland are exposed to air and

rapidly oxidize the organic material that had been trapped. The result is that thousands of years of accumulated organic material is released into the water system and atmosphere in a relatively short time.

The removal of dams (human-made or beaver-made) lowers the water level (i.e. drains) above the dam and can have severe downstream impacts beyond the effects of increased nutrients released from oxidizing organic soils. Dam removal (even small scale beaver dam removal) typically results in increased downstream flow which causes bank erosion and scouring, and the release of silt and sediment that had been trapped behind the dam. The combination of erosion, scouring, and increased sediment load can have devastating effects on the ability of a stream to support desirable aquatic life. Thus, although dam removal is usually done in the name of fisheries habitat improvement, it can often cause more damage than good to the aquatic system.

Land Use Changes

Land use changes in the watershed can affect how a wetland functions. With respect to changes in hydrology, the most typical land use changes are those which involve the conversion of natural vegetation or farmland to areas in which much of the land surface is covered with impervious surfaces (roofs, pavement, etc.). The changes to wetland hydrology are twofold: 1) a reduction in the amount of precipitation that can percolate into the soil and then be discharged slowly into a wetland as ground water, and 2) a dramatic increase in the amount of water that flows into a wetland via surface water. Both of these combine to create a situation where the major inputs of water become "flashy," causing the amplitude of the fluctuations between high water and low water in the wetland to become more extreme. An additional concern is the presence of sediment, nutrients, and other pollutants in stormwater runoff. Although wetlands do serve as natural filters, the amount of pollutants in urban stormwater runoff is typically greater than what wetlands can

handle. This degraded water quality can severely impact wetland functions. Like other changes in wetland hydrology, the result is a change in vegetation community, wildlife habitat, and the ability of the wetland to serve critical functions such as flood storage and water quality protection.

Dredging

Dredging activities are those in which the soil surface in a wetland is changed by the removal of soil. This can involve such large-scale projects as the dredging of a ditch, canal, or harbor, or such small-scale projects as grading an undulating wetland for the purpose of landscaping a lawn. Dredging disturbs and removes the vegetation and soil of a wetland. This topographic change (even in small scale projects) essentially changes the hydrology of the wetland by making the surface either closer to the water table or under deeper water. Since dredging involves removal of organic accumulations and exposure of the underlaying subsoil, dredging activities usually result in a wetland substrate less able to support vegetation and other aquatic life. Again, the result is a change in vegetation community, wildlife habitat, and other functions. In addition, by disturbing wetland soils, especially those in direct contact with water bodies, dredging activities release sediment into receiving waters. This can be especially damaging in cases where the soils contain contaminants.

A common dredging activity in intact wetlands is for the purpose of creating ponds or open water in an otherwise pondless wetland. This is commonly done with the intent of improving or "enhancing" wetlands. Although a shallow pond is a type of wetland (aquatic bed), it does not necessarily follow that all wetlands should have ponds, or that a pond is always an enhancement. When a pond is dredged in a wetland that does not otherwise have open water, some functions associated with the original wetland are changed or lost. In some cases, where wetlands have been degraded by past activities (such as intensive livestock grazing and subsequent invasion by nuisance species), dredging a shallow pond may be a valuable management activity. To serve as effective wildlife habitat, ponds associated with wetlands should be shallow with gently sloping sides, an undulating bottom, and a sinuous edge. All spoils from pond construction should be moved to a suitable upland site and stabilized to control erosion. It is important to note that pond construction, like other dredging activities, requires a wetland permit.

Filling

Past wetland filling activities in Michigan have ranged from large-scale filling of wetlands to provide suitable conditions for constructing buildings, to small-scale filling to plant grass in one's front yard. The result of both activities is essentially the same: change in the soils, hydrology, and vegetation of an area from wetland to upland. Accordingly, the wetland's natural functions are lost. Furthermore, unlike activities such as drainage which may provide opportunities for wetland restoration, once land is converted to upland by filling, it is usually a permanent change. Obviously, landowners concerned about protecting their wetlands would not want to engage in large-scale filling. However, the impacts of small-scale filling activities are often overlooked. Two small-scale filling activities that have substantial adverse impacts on wetlands, but are common among landowners, include landscaping for lawns and building bulkheads.

Many landowners who construct a home on lakefront property desire to have a "lawn to the lake." If the property has wetlands bordering the lake, or other body of water, fulfilling this desire usually involves filling the wetland fringe (or at least grading the high spots into the low spots—essentially dredging and filling). Next, nonnative turfgrass is planted and typically maintained with unnecessarily high doses of pesticides and fertilizers. The result is a loss of fish and wildlife habitat, a reduction in water quality due to the increase in polluted runoff and the destruction of the natural filtering capacity of the shoreline wetland, an increase in erosion potential due to the removal of shoreline wetland plants, and a loss of the aesthetic values of the wetland.

An activity often associated with creating the "lawn to the lake" is the creation of bulkheads or seawalls. Ironically, most seawalls are proposed for the purpose of controlling erosion—erosion which many times is a direct result of destroying the natural vegetation along the shoreline. Wetlands along the shoreline of lakes, rivers, and streams (called riparian wetlands) provide especially important nursery habitat for fish and other aquatic life. They also play an important role as pollutant filters for runoff entering surface water. Bulkheads are typically proposed to be built in this critical zone of aquatic habitat. As a result, the important functions that these wetlands provide are directly lost. They are also indirectly lost as a result of the bulkhead's effect on wave activity and water flow patterns on adjacent and nearby shorelines (which can cause either sediment deposition or shoreline erosion).

In addition to the mechanical filling described above, the dark history of how we have treated wetlands involves another type of filling—that of dumping rubbish into wetlands. Since wetlands have traditionally been viewed as wastelands, they have unfortunately been used as dumps. Old cars, refrigerators, stoves, tires, bikes, and every other imaginable household waste item can be found in wetlands. In addition to the unsightly nature of this sort of filling, some of these items may have released toxic substances into the wetland. Refuse should be removed from wetlands, and neighbors and other likely "dumpers" should be educated about the importance of wetland protection. A great way to educate people is to invite them

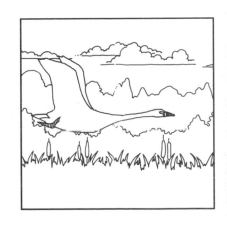

to help remove the garbage in a neighborhood clean-up project.

Another common dumping practice is to throw lawn clippings, wood chips, and other yard waste into wetlands. This is often done with the intent of filling the wetland, perhaps to extend a lawn or garden area. Any kind of filling results in a loss of wetland functions. Additionally, dumping yard waste could cause changes in a wetland's chemical balance. Yard waste is composed of natural materials that will eventually decompose. As they decompose they release nutrients and use up oxygen that is necessary for aquatic life. The best thing to do with yard waste is to compost it at a reasonable distance away from the wetland or other water body.

Vegetation Clearing

Although vegetation clearing (including forestry activities) is technically exempt from wetland protection statutes, the effect on wetland functions can be extremely damaging. For the most part, the vegetation in a wetland provides the wildlife habitat. Through evapotranspiration, nutrient uptake, and the physical structure of rooted plants, vegetation influences hydrology and is critical to a wetland's ability to protect water quality, control soil erosion, and control floods. In addition, depending on the actual method and equipment used, vegetation clearing can cause severe erosion and sedimentation. Some landowners clear vegetation because they think that it may dry the site out. In fact, because trees and other vegetation facilitate the removal of water through evapotranspiration, vegetation clearing can make the land more wet.

Humans are not the only animals that clear wetland vegetation. In many parts of the state, wetlands are used as summer pasture for cattle. When livestock graze in wetlands the typical result is trampled banks, damaged vegetation, and direct addition of animal waste to the aquatic system. Such a degraded system quickly ceases to perform its natural functions and is ripe for being overtaken by such invasive species as reed-canary grass.

In some cases, vegetation clearing can be a useful method to maintain a certain type of wetland. For instance, if there is a need to maintain a wet prairie for the purpose of providing habitat for threatened or endangered plant species, then active management techniques (e.g., controlled burn) to impede invasion by woody species (which would turn the prairie into shrub swamp) may be desirable. Another example may be to cut "marsh hay" from a wetland to maintain its wet meadow character for the benefit of birds like pheasant that use such areas for feeding and cover.

Exotic and Nuisance Species Invasion

Introduction of exotic (nonnative) plants has damaged ecosystems around the world. Exotic plants choke out native vegetation and alter the way wetlands function. This can affect sediment removal, nutrient uptake, fish and wildlife habitat, and other functions. Exotic plants are introduced to wetlands either directly, as decorative additions, or indirectly through natural seeding from exotics placed in nearby lawns and gardens. Nuisance (or weed) plants can be native species that outcompete other native species under certain conditions.

Purple loosestrife is the most striking example of an exotic plant impacting wetlands. Due to its amazing reproductive capabilities (it is a perennial plant that can spread by its roots and produces between 100,000 and 2 million seeds each year), and the fact that it has neither parasites nor diseases in this country, it can literally take over wetland vegetation communities. Unfortunately, few wildlife species find the purple loosestrife palatable. Wetlands that once contained diverse vegetation communities and provided excellent wildlife habitat are now monotypic stands of purple loosestrife and seemingly devoid of animal life.

Because the large reddish-purple flower heads are admittedly beautiful, many people have purposefully planted purple loosestrife in their wetlands and flower gardens. Thus, people have actively facilitated its spread. Attempts to control the spread of this plant have met with very little success—especially in areas where it has become well established. In response to the impacts of this plant on the functions of Michigan's wetlands, the Michigan Legislature passed a law that outlaws the retail sale of purple loosestrife in Michigan.

Using Chemicals

Fertilizers and pesticides (plant and insect killers) represent a potential threat to your wetland. If they are used on adjacent or upstream lawns or farmland it is likely they will eventually enter local waterways and your wetland. Additional nutrients from fertilizers (especially phosphorus) can upset the natural balance in the wetland system and cause extensive plant and algae growth in adjacent water bodies. Likewise, pesticides and herbicides can upset the natural flora and fauna of a wetland by impacting the ability of some plants or animals to survive. On a positive note, selective use of herbicides can have a beneficial use in controlling exotic species.

Recreational Overuse

Off road vehicles (ORVs)—dirt bikes, all-terrain vehicles, and mountain bikes—destroy soils, vegetation, and wildlife habitat within your wetland and its adjacent upland. The unwise use of motorboats and personal watercrafts (i.e. "jet-skis") can disrupt wildlife and wetlands located along the shores of rivers, lakes, and streams. Boat wakes can disturb nesting waterfowl, especially the Common Loon, and cause severe shoreline erosion in heavy recreational use areas.

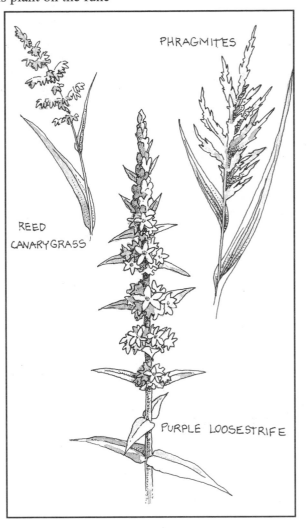

MANAGEMENT PRACTICES TO PROTECT WETLANDS

The simplest way to manage your wetland to protect it from the activities above is simply not to engage in them. In addition, many landowners want to engage in low impact enhancement activities or do more to ensure that their wetlands are protected for the long term. All too often our thoughts about what we can do to protect wetlands is limited to activities within the wetland. As we saw in the threats to wetlands listed above, many activities that can severely impact wetlands are generated by activities outside of the wetland, often many miles away. Accordingly, the management activities that landowners can take to guard their wetlands can occur outside the wetland boundaries. Below you will find brief descriptions of many activities that you can do on your property to protect your wetlands and improve wildlife habitat. The intention is to provide you with enough information to know that a particular management activity is possible. Obtaining additional information on how to implement the activity (e.g., designing and planting a greenbelt) is recommended.

Install Nest Boxes and Platforms

One popular reason why people own wetlands is because of the bountiful wildlife habitat they provide. It follows then that most landowners who want to actively manage their property do so for the purpose of enhancing the area for

wildlife. One of the most critical components of wildlife habitat is the availability of safe nesting areas. For ground nesters such as the mallard, wetlands that have no upland buffer provide little opportunity for nesting. For cavity nesters such as the wood duck and hooded merganser, the removal of large trees and snags adjacent to and in wetlands has severely limited their nesting opportunities. Landowners who want to create nesting areas for these and other species can build nest boxes, cylinders, and platforms and place them in appropriate locations in their wetland. Installing nest boxes involves a commitment to the birds using them. Unless you are willing to maintain the nest box or cylinder annually (i.e., clean out and replace wood shavings), it is best not to install them at all.

Boxes on posts or trees should be placed 4 to 5 feet above water surfaces and 15 to 30 feet above land surfaces. Boxes should be placed so that the entrance hole is visible to ducks on the water. Nesting platforms placed in the water should be at least 50 feet from the shoreline to reduce predation. Ducks using boxes are more prone to predation than those using natural cavities. Human scent on trees and nest structures is an attractant to predators such as raccoons, opossum, and skunks. To ensure that the nest boxes that you put up do not serve to feed the local raccoon population, do not place nest boxes without using adequate predator guards.

In addition to waterfowl, dozens of other birds use wetlands for nesting and feeding. Tree swallows will readily nest in constructed boxes, and their aerial gymnastics are very entertaining. Because their main source of food is flying insects, they can also provide much appreciated mosquito control. The same is true for the several species of Michigan's flying mammals—bats. Up to 36 little

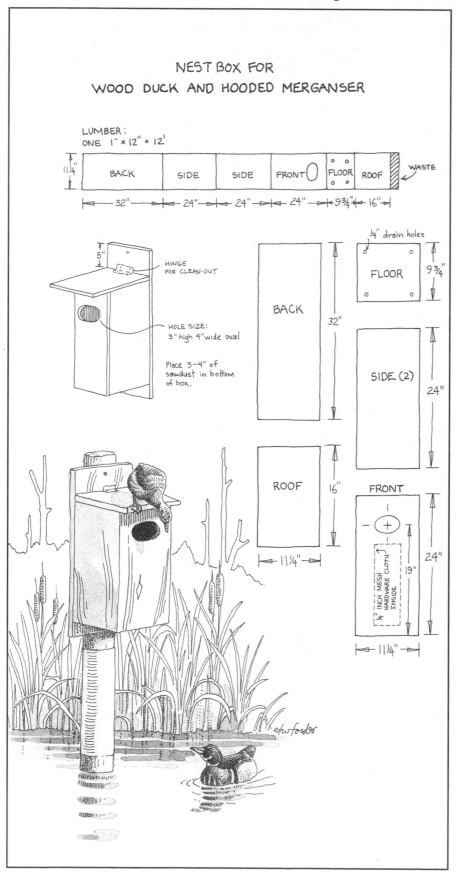

brown bats will roost in one bat house. Each night, a colony of this size eats thousands of insects.

Establish and Maintain Buffers or Greenbelts

Perhaps the most effective management practice to protect wetlands from adjacent human activities is to establish and maintain a vegetative buffer (or greenbelt) around the wetland. A greenbelt is simply a strip of upland surrounding

the wetland that is maintained in a natural vegetated state. On properties which have had the natural vegetation removed, establishing a greenbelt involves planting native trees, shrubs, and ground cover, ceasing use of fertilizers and pesticides, and only cutting or removing select vegetation.

Greenbelts around wetlands provide many valuable functions. The vegetation in the greenbelt uptakes excess nutrients and pollutants in overland flow and thereby protects the wetland. The vegetation also serves to slow the velocity of overland flow which helps to prevent erosion and creates a better opportunity for the water to percolate into the soils. This helps to reduce the "flashy" nature of runoff from urbanized areas. Greenbelts are very important from a wildlife standpoint. The greenbelt serves as a visual and noise barrier to the interior of the wetland, which is beneficial to wildlife that are sensitive to human disturbance. The greenbelt also serves as a habitat connector between the wetland and upland habitats, or as a protective pathway between different wetlands. Such wildlife corridors are very important to many animals, especially those with large ranges. In addition, greenbelts can be valuable habitat in their own right for animals that periodically use the wetland but spend most of their time in nearby uplands. Such habitat can be enhanced by select planting and maintenance without any adverse effect on the other functions of the greenbelt.

The ideal greenbelt width ranges from 50 to 300 feet or more depending on a variety of factors, including slope, soil type, amount of water flowing through the

What to Plant In Your Greenbelt

In an area where only grass or other ground cover exists, simply not mowing will begin natural vegetation succession which will result in a variety of trees, woody shrubs, and herbaceous ground cover. However, natural succession can take many years to reestablish an effective greenbelt. If you want to speed up the process, consider planting the following species.

Trees	Woody shrubs	Herbaceous Ground Cover
Dry, Well-drained (Upland) Soils		
red pine	beaked hazelnut	baneberry
hemlock	mountain maple	large-leafed aster
sugar maple	striped maple	bunchberry
white birch	native honeysuckles	Canada mayflower
white spruce	staghorn sumac	blackberry or raspberry
American beech	juniper	bearberry
red oak	ninebark	bracken fern
white pine	buffalo berry	partridge berry
aspen	flowering dogwood	wintergreen
		goldenrod
Wet, Poorly Drained (Wetland) Soils		
northern white cedar	red-osier dogwood	boneset
tamarack	silky dogwood	joe-pye weed
red maple	willows	cordgrass
green ash	meadow sweet	sedges and rushes
black willow	winterberry	royal fern
balsam fir	American black currant	mint
balsam poplar	sweet gale	sweet flag
	alder	cattail
	button bush	Canada anemone
	high bush cranberry	blue flag iris
		virgins bower

greenbelt, size of wetland, functions the wetland provides, activities in the watershed, and management goals such as attracting certain types of wildlife into the greenbelt area. Even if you cannot install a greenbelt of the ideal width, it is important to remember that a greenbelt of any width is better than no greenbelt at all.

Protect and Enhance Adjacent Upland Habitat

What happens in your wetland is influenced by what happens in the upland parts of your wetland's watershed. The establishment and maintenance of a greenbelt is considered the first line of defense against pollutant-laden stormwater and as a buffer against upland activity that might adversely impact the wetland. However, just as a wetland can be over stressed by too much sediment and nutrient input, greenbelts cannot be expected to handle the stormwater, sediment, and other pollutants resulting from poor land use management activities in adjacent uplands.

Most wetland wildlife, including many waterfowl species, benefit from upland nesting and feeding areas adjacent to wetlands. Ground nesting species such as mallard and black ducks require either uplands adjacent to wetlands, nesting islands, or artificial platforms. Establishing native vegetation in the upland around your wetland can meet the needs of these and numerous other wildlife species. Songbirds, raptors (such as the threatened red-shouldered hawk and bald eagle), and game birds such as woodcock, pheasant, and ruffed grouse all benefit from undeveloped uplands adjacent to wetlands. For recommendations on what plant species should be established to attract certain types of wildlife, contact your County Soil and Water Conservation District, groups that focus on a particular species (e.g., Pheasants Forever or Ducks Unlimited), or other conservation organization that provide landowner assistance.

Managing stormwater runoff to protect water quality also benefits wildlife. Wetland animals such as frogs and other amphibians are very sensitive to changes in water quality—more so than most other wetland animals. Since amphibians are an important component in the wetland food web, activities that impact amphibians will impact other animals such as fish, herons, and mink.

How you protect and enhance adjacent upland habitat will depend on your unique circumstances and primary management goals (e.g., stormwater management or black duck nesting habitat). Accordingly, there is no practical way to address the wide range of options in this chapter. Regardless of what you are planning to do in the uplands (e.g., nothing, farm corn, build homes, etc.), there are several things that you must keep in mind: How can I manage stormwater runoff so that its quantity is as close as possible to the original flow? What pollutants might my upland activities be generating and how can I control them on site? What wildlife use the upland/wetland complex and how can I manage the uplands to benefit these species? Once these questions are answered, how to manage the uplands to benefit your wetland will become more clear.

Install Fencing

In areas where livestock grazing in wetlands or excessive human use (e.g., ORV use) is degrading wetlands, fencing is one of the simplest ways to protect your wetland. This is especially critical in wetlands along streams and lakes where the degradation is directly impacting water quality through erosion and sedimentation. Even if you can't fence all of your wetland, you can often fence off overused places where extra protection is necessary. There are several things to consider when determining what fencing is best for you. First, fencing should be placed as far from the wetland as is reasonably possible. In this way, the fenced area also includes a protective buffer between the activity and the wetland. Second, choosing the correct fence material for the purpose will save money and maintenance time. For example, a single-strand, high-tensile fence with flexible line posts will keep cattle out of an area, will collect less debris, and is less likely to be damaged during flooding than a woven wire fence.

Control Stormwater Runoff

Runoff is an important component of a wetland's hydrologic budget. However, what stormwater picks up from the ground surface on its way to the wetland can be damaging, especially in urban areas. In an undeveloped vegetated landscape a majority of the precipitation soaks into the ground and becomes ground water. In areas that are urbanized, much of the ground is covered with impervious surfaces such as roofs and concrete. As a result, there is an increase in the quantity and a decrease in the quality of water entering the wetland. There are three primary issues

related to stormwater runoff that landowners must consider when protecting wetlands. The first is to minimize the amount of stormwater runoff that is generated beyond background levels. The second is to consider where and how to convey the stormwater. The third is to refrain from activities that pollute stormwater runoff.

The best way to minimize stormwater is to minimize the amount of impervious surfaces that cover the ground. For projects that will generate runoff no matter what you do (like building the roof of a house), it is best to do what you can to encourage the water to soak into the ground, thus minimizing the runoff that leaves the site and enters the wetland. If enough runoff is generated so that it must be conveyed somewhere, then the best option is to construct a grass-lined swale. The grass will help to slow runoff so it does not cause erosion, the living plants will take up nutrients, and the physical structure of the plants will help trap sediments. The specific design of a grass swale will depend on slope, soils, and amount of runoff. Environmental consultants or your local Soil and Water Conservation District staff can help you design a grass-lined swale that meets your needs. The *Guidebook of Best Management Practices for Michigan Watersheds*, available from the Michigan Department of Environmental Quality, also provides useful advise.

The third issue noted above deals with being conscious of the fact that what we put on the land ends up in our water. Every year in Michigan, millions of gallons of oil are still poured on the ground during "do-it-yourself" oil changes. This oil then ends up contaminating ground water. Pesticides and herbicides flow off the land with the water and enter our wetlands, lakes, and streams. What we put on the ground around our home or farm ends up in our drinking water or surface water. Before you decide to dump something on the ground, ask yourself, "Is this something that I would want to drink or swim in?"

A common source of pollutants to stormwater that deserves special note is the area around the garage and driveway. In the garage we have petroleum products and other chemicals that are used for household and car maintenance projects. Many of these compounds are considered hazardous. If you let these products drain into the floor drain, onto the driveway, or the down the storm drain at the curb, they will eventually wash into local waterways. If you have household hazardous waste that you'd like to have disposed of properly, contact your local health department, recycling center, or MSU Extension office to find out about local hazardous waste collection and disposal opportunities.

Maintain Septic Systems

Septic systems also are a source of pollutants to wetlands. Be sure your septic system is operating properly. If you notice the area over your drain field is wet or particularly green, or if you can smell sewage during rainy periods, then your system is not working properly. Seepage from your system may be polluting nearby areas, including your wetland. To avoid this problem, have your septic system pumped and inspected every three to five years (or less, depending on the system) and commit to upgrading the system when necessary. In addition, water conservation practices such as installing low-flow toilets and shower heads can extend the life of a septic system.

Use Fertilizers and Pesticides Wisely

There are many safe alternatives to chemical fertilizers and pesticides around the home. Organic pesticide formulations, use of other insects to fight pests, and composting kitchen and yard waste to enrich soil have all been successful in meeting the needs of homeowners. The MSU Extension Agent in your county and many environmental organizations can recommend alternatives to using chemical fertilizers and pesticides. Many homeowners use fertilizers when they do not need to. Before you decide to use fertilizers, you should get your soil tested to see if it is even necessary. If you do use fertilizers or pesticides, follow manufacturer's directions carefully. Never apply more than is recommended. On the farm, use pesticides, herbicides, and fertilizers only when needed and within product guide-lines. Research into the technology and practice of Integrated Pest Management (IPM) has provided an excellent way to reduce reliance on heavy inputs of pesti-cides. Contact the NRCS, your Soil and Water Conservation District, or MSU Extension Agent to find out about IPM practices in your area. The establishment of a chemical-free greenbelt to buffer the wetland from upland use of fertilizers and pesticides is very important.

Manage Recreational Use

Waves from motorboats can cause erosion damage to riparian wetlands. Although wetlands serve to dampen wave energy, the waves from boats often gener-ate much larger waves than the physical parameters of the water body would normally generate. One way to protect these areas is to establish "No Wake Zones." In other cases, it may be appropri-ate to limit the speed or motor size on an entire lake. To find out how to establish a no wake zone near your wetland or a speed limit on your lake, contact the marine division of your county sheriff's office. Because of the damage to soils and vegeta-tion, the use of ORVs such as dirt bikes, all-terrain vehicles, and even mountain bikes should not be permitted in wetlands.

Recreational activities such as hunting, fishing, hiking, canoeing, and bird watch-ing are compatible with wetland protection as long as wildlife and their habitat are not disturbed by overuse. If you and your family and friends are the only individuals using the wetland, then recreation activities are not likely to be a problem. How-ever, if you have many other individuals using your land who may not be sensitive to the needs of wildlife, then you may need to limit some uses during critical times such as breeding or nesting seasons. Accomplishing this might be as simple as a sign at access points or something more complicated like installing a fence or constructing a boardwalk to manage where people go in the wetland.

Control Pets

Your "gentle" house pets can wreak havoc on the wildlife populations you may be trying to protect. Dogs can seriously harass wetland species. Cats are very effective predators, especially on young animals. Declawing house cats somewhat reduces their ability to kill small animals. Both cats and dogs should be restricted from the wetland during the spring and summer nesting season: Keeping your dog on a leash allows access to the wetland yet eliminates wildlife harassment.

Beaver Management

As noted above, beavers can be a very important component of wetland systems. However, they can also be a nuisance. The most important part of beaver management is population regulation. Beavers have one or two kits each year. An established beaver colony is usually composed of three generations: kits, yearlings, and a pair of adults. When the yearlings become two-year-olds, they usually leave the parental colony to set up their own colony elsewhere, which makes room for the next litter of kits. An established colony of beavers can sustain the removal of between one and two beavers each year. If fewer beavers are removed, then colonization of additional habitat will occur and the chances for nuisance beaver activity will increase.

The removal of established dams should be avoided unless it is determined necessary for the benefit of the river or stream system by a competent biologist. Even then, beaver dam removal should be done slowly and carefully to avoid downstream scouring from increased flows and to reduce downstream siltation. It should also be noted that beaver dam removal will not solve the problems associated with beavers unless the activity is coupled with beaver removal.

A different solution to beaver dam removal that does not have the negative effects of stream siltation or bank scouring is the installation of a Clemson Beaver

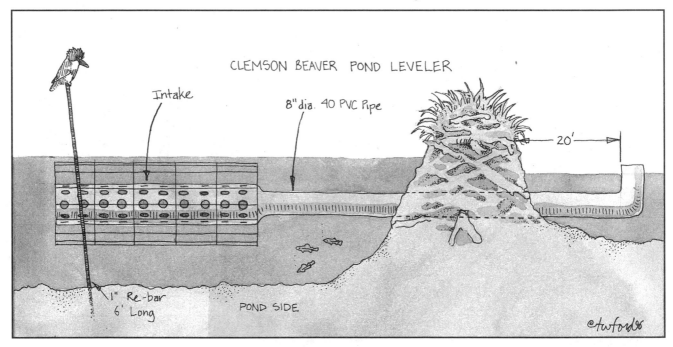

Pond Leveler. This simple device, also known as a "Beaver Fooler," is essentially a large tube (8-inch diameter PVC pipe) that is placed through the beaver dam. Both ends of the pipe are constructed so that the beavers are not able to clog the inlet or outlet. If the landowner desires to maintain some of the pond behind the dam, the Beaver Fooler can be constructed to maintain a certain water level upstream of the dam. Since beavers occupy streams and rivers that flow across lands owned by many different individuals, it is important to coordinate beaver management activities with neighboring landowners.

Control Shoreline Erosion

In shoreline areas that are experiencing erosion, controlling erosion is very important. The first step in controlling erosion is to evaluate the nature and extent of the problem and determine if the problem is serious enough to warrant corrective action. There are two basic reasons for controlling erosion: to protect property and to protect the environment. If the erosion is largely the result of natural processes that do not harm the environment and that do not threaten property, then erosion control may not be necessary. Assuming that you determine that the nature and extent of the erosion warrant corrective measures, the next step is to look at the alternative methods of control and select the one most appropriate.

The traditional method of controlling erosion is to construct a bulkhead at the water's edge or armor the shoreline with rock riprap. Such activities often result in the loss of wetland habitat and can exacerbate erosion problems for adjacent landowners. Researchers have developed an environmentally friendly, aesthetically pleasing, and effective method of controlling shoreline erosion that relies on the use of vegetation (both living and nonliving) and is known as biotechnical erosion control (BEC). In its simplest terms, BEC involves the reestablishment of a diverse vegetation community that mimics a natural shoreline system. The vegetation at the shoreline, and in the water itself, binds the soil and provides increased protection against erosion. With careful vegetation trimming you can have a pleasing filtered view of the wetland, lake, or stream while still maintaining a naturally stable vegetated shoreline.

Be Aware of Activities in Your Watershed

The quality of your wetland reflects the quality of the watershed that provides its lifeblood. Be aware of proposed and ongoing activities in your watershed that could adversely impact the quality of your wetland. Activities might include new residential or commercial development, roads, sewers, or other infrastructure, or the establishment and maintenance of agricultural drains. If you identify a proposed activity that will impact your wetland, contact the person or agencies proposing it to find out more and discuss alternatives that would have less impact on your land. If this is not successful, it may be necessary to participate in the decision-making process at the local, state, or federal level by going to meetings, providing public comment, and sharing your information with other neighbors. To find out about proposed activities, contact your local environmental or conservation group. In addition, the Land and Water Management Division of the MDEQ distributes a biweekly list of wetland permit applications submitted to the MDEQ.

Control Exotic and Nuisance Species

Management activities to control the spread or invasion of exotic plant species which impact wetland vegetation communities and wildlife habitat vary depending on the size and type of the wetland, the invading species, the extent of the invasion, and the resources available to the landowner. The most ubiquitous exotic or nuisance plant species impacting Michigan's wetlands are reed canary grass, buckthorn (common and glossy), phragmites, and purple loosestrife. The worst of these is purple loosestrife. Although each of these plants looks different, they share many similarities. They have few pests, they form dense stands which crowd out other vegetation, and they have little value as food or cover for native wildlife.

The first and best line of defense is to minimize the opportunities for invasion by nuisance species. Landowners should refrain from growing invasive species in their yards or gardens and should discourage their neighbors from doing so also.

Given that plant seeds can be transported into your wetland by other sources (flowing water, birds and other animals, etc.), it will not be possible to stop all introduction of exotic and nuisance species into your wetland. Accordingly, the next line of defense is to destroy those plants that do make it into your wetland and take root. If the introduced population is small, and they are recognized and removed early, there is a good chance that you can keep your wetland from being completely overrun. Removal methods include hand pulling or cutting the vegetation before the seeds set and cautious use of herbicides that affect broadleaved plant species. Hand pulling may require gently "teasing" the roots to facilitate pulling the

entire plant. Although hand pulling involves the most time, some consider it the most effective way to eradicate new stands.

Vegetation cutting alone will limit seed production and dramatically slow the spread of a loosestrife or phragmites stand, but it will not remove it. This is because invasive plants like purple loosestrife and phragmites can reproduce from the root stock. In addition, purple loosestrife can sprout from plant pieces. For this reason, it is important to be careful to remove all plant pieces from the wetland when hand pulling or cutting these species.

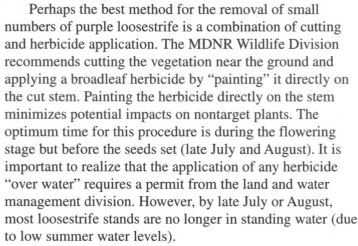

Perhaps the best method for the removal of small numbers of purple loosestrife is a combination of cutting and herbicide application. The MDNR Wildlife Division recommends cutting the vegetation near the ground and applying a broadleaf herbicide by "painting" it directly on the cut stem. Painting the herbicide directly on the stem minimizes potential impacts on nontarget plants. The optimum time for this procedure is during the flowering stage but before the seeds set (late July and August). It is important to realize that the application of any herbicide "over water" requires a permit from the land and water management division. However, by late July or August, most loosestrife stands are no longer in standing water (due to low summer water levels).

In 1994, the MDNR Wildlife Division released two species of European leaf-eating beetles to field test a biological control of purple loosestrife at three sites. The beetles have been shown to be highly selective for feeding on purple loosestrife. The natural interaction of the leaf-eating beetles, along with other insects, effectively controls purple loosestrife outbreaks in Europe. The beetles attack the plant by feeding on stems, flowers, and leaves, which weakens the plants and gives competing native plants a chance to grow. It is not yet known whether these beetles will be effective in Michigan and available for use by private landowners.

Work With Your Neighbors

Although this guidebook is written with the individual landowner in mind, it's obvious that the land use decisions made by other landowners, businesses, and governments influence the functions and values of the wetland on your property. In addition, the boundaries of most wetlands extend beyond the property lines of the individual property owner. Because of this, multiple landowners share in the responsibility to maintain the ecological integrity of the wetland ecosystem. By learning more about your wetland, the activities which impact its functions, and different ways to protect your wetland, you are in a good position to help yourself and your neighbors better manage the wetland that you have in common. Share the information in this chapter with your neighbor. Help provide him or her with alternatives to activities that degrade wetlands. Together you will both be able to maintain the benefits that wetlands naturally provide for the long term.

Each of the topics in this chapter could fill a guidebook of its own. The purpose here was to provide you with an awareness of the range of things you can do to protect your wetland. If you desire additional information or want to pursue some of the more complicated activities, contact one of the resource agencies or conservation organizations listed in the appendices.

Wetlands Restoration, Enhancement and Creation

CHAPTER 8

WHY RESTORE, ENHANCE, OR CREATE WETLANDS?

Michigan has lost approximately half of its original wetlands. Despite their numerous functions and values and the realization that they are ecologically vital, wetlands continue to be lost. We can reverse this trend by restoring wetlands which have been degraded and creating new wetlands when conditions are appropriate.

Historically, most wetlands were destroyed by draining for agricultural purposes. Land that has been effectively drained and successfully farmed in the past may be too wet in some years to produce a good crop. In these areas, the best use of that land may be to restore its original wetland hydrology and allow it to once again become a fully functioning wetland.

In Michigan, wetlands have formed in the landscape over thousands of years—since the last retreat of the glaciers. Given this, it is understandable that restoration or creation of a wetland that "totally duplicates" a naturally occurring wetland is practically impossible due to the complexity and variation in wetland ecosystems. Some systems, however, may be approximated and individual wetland functions may be restored or created. Flood storage, waterfowl habitat, and recreational open space are easiest to restore. Forested wetlands, ground water discharge and recharge, delicate food chain relationships, and habitat for endangered species are more difficult.

At one time, it was thought that natural wetlands were good places to discharge wastewater because of their capacity for treating wastes. It is now apparent that the natural waste treatment function of a wetland can be over stressed by inputs of excessive pollutants. Artificial wetlands, however, are being successfully designed and constructed to treat wastewater. These systems are typically constructed in a way that allows for periodic removal of pollutants trapped by the created wetland. To date, thousands of wetlands have been created for treatment of human sewage, agricultural and industrial waste, urban runoff, and acid mine drainage. Many

wetlands have also been created to mitigate for losses due to permitted wetland degradation. From these efforts have come much of our present knowledge about techniques for wetland creation and restoration.

DEFINITIONS

Terms like wetland restoration, enhancement, and creation mean different things to different people. For the purposes of this discussion, commonly accepted definitions are noted below. In this chapter the term wetland project is used as a general term to refer to restoration, enhancement, and creation projects.

Wetland Restoration is a term used to describe activities that seek to return wetlands to a previously existing natural condition from a disturbed or totally altered state. It is not necessary to have complete knowledge of what the preexisting conditions were. Rather, it is enough to know a wetland of whatever type was there and have as a goal the return to that same wetland type. Most wetlands were converted to uplands by ditching, tiling, stream channelization, or other hydrologic manipulation. Drained sites will retain hydric soils and likely retain a wetland vegetation seed bank for many decades. Wetland hydrology can often be restored by plugging drainage ditches, or by removing segments of drain tile. If the original wetland hydrology can be restored, then the site can again become a functioning wetland.

Wetland Enhancement is the improvement, maintenance, and management of existing wetlands for a particular function or value, possibly at the expense of others. For the purposes of this book, wetland enhancement activities are divided into two categories: high impact and management. High impact enhancement involves changing the physical characteristic of the wetland from what it was historically. Examples of high impact enhancement activity include dredging to create a pond for waterfowl in a wetland that currently does not have open water, or impounding water at a greater depth or duration than what occurred historically. High impact activities usually require permits and result in enhancing one wetland function at the expense of others. Management activities are those which do not involve changes in soils or hydrology of wetlands. Examples of management (or low impact enhancement) activities include installing nest boxes or platforms for waterfowl, controlling the spread of exotic species such as purple loosestrife, maintaining greenbelts around wetlands, and planting upland habitat with food cover. These and other management activities are addressed in Chapter 7.

Wetland Creation is the conversion of an area that was historically upland into a wetland. Wetlands are most commonly created by impounding water or excavating surface soils. This usually involves intensive, costly efforts, such as earth movement and vegetation planting. The most common, successfully created wetlands have been shallow impoundments and shallow excavations in areas adjacent to existing wetlands where the ground water table was already fairly close to the soil surface. In these situations, hydrology and wetland vegetation can often be easily established and revegetation can occur quickly. As a general rule, created wetlands do not function as well as restored wetlands. Furthermore, wetland creation is the most expensive of the three processes and has the greatest chance for failure.

TECHNIQUES FOR RESTORATION, HIGH IMPACT ENHANCEMENT, AND CREATION

Although some general guidelines have been developed over the years, the science of wetland restoration and creation is still quite new and wetland restoration, enhancement, and creation activities and opportunities are so diverse, that it is not possible (nor desired) to develop simple and rigid "cookbook" guidance for wetland restoration, creation, or enhancement. If you are interested in doing a wetland restoration, high-impact enhancement, or creation project, it is recommended that you contact one of the many conservation organizations, agencies, or consultants who provide services to landowners in this arena. Chapter 10 and the appendices provide information on available programs and organizations.

To give you an idea of what might be involved with a restoration, high impact enhancement, or creation activity, below are some general steps which should be considered for any wetland project.

Step 1 - Identification of Goals and Site Selection
Identify the Goals of Your Wetland Project.

Which wetland functions and values would you like your wetland to possess? The size and shape of the wetland will be largely determined by its purpose. If the wetland is for waterfowl habitat, then an irregular shoreline with a mixture of islands, open water, and dense emergent vegetation will be best. If the wetland is for waste treatment purposes, then long, narrow, straight-sided "cells" that can be cleaned out are often best.

Evaluate the Site

Evaluate the site(s) under consideration to help determine the feasibility of the project and to be sure it will provide an adequate setting for your goals. The most important information includes soil type, watershed features (size, slope, water availability, water quality), existing vegetation cover types, adjacent land uses, property boundaries, and evaluation of fish and wildlife habitat (including threatened and endangered species). Areas that were former wetlands provide the most successful opportunities for wetland restoration. If you are not intimately familiar with a prospective piece of property, this information can be obtained by reviewing soil surveys, topographic maps, resource maps prepared by local, state, or federal agencies, health department well logs, and a general on-site inspection.

Secure Necessary Permits

Based on your goals for the project and the proposed site, you should know at this stage of the process what permits may be needed. A permit will be needed when dredging, filling, draining, or construction occurs in regulated wetlands or legally established drains. Before commencing a project, check with the Michigan Department of Environmental Quality, U. S. Army Corps of Engineers, the county drain commissioner, and local units of government to determine which permits will be required. Considering and addressing permitting concerns early in the project planning phase is very important. If you are planning a restoration project and you have a drain on your property, you must first determine if it is a designated drain under jurisdiction of the county drain commissioner. If it is a designated drain, find out if there are any maintenance or expansion plans, and if so, what impact these plans will have on your project.

Step 2 - Detailed Project Planning

Wetland projects can be designed with a variety of shapes, sizes, degrees of wetness, and biogeochemical characteristics. Except in very small, simple projects, a detailed planning and design stage is essential before beginning construction. Wetland projects that involve the construction of berms or water level control structures should be designed and constructed according to civil engineering standards to provide reliability, safety, and reasonable cost. Additional collection of detailed data will probably be necessary in this step in order to complete the project design. In general, the larger the project, the more information will be necessary to ensure that the project is adequately designed and implemented. The following basic information should be compiled when designing wetland projects.

Topography

Detailed topographic drawings showing existing and proposed contour intervals, property boundaries, prominent physical features, and the boundaries of the wetland should be made. Wetlands can actually be created in most upland areas where water supply is adequate and slopes are not too steep, but the construction may be expensive and more likely to fail.

Soils

By boring, determine the types of different soils and their extent, and the depth to ground water. Construction is easiest on low permeability soils (e.g., clay) because little water will be lost to infiltration. If native soils are permeable, some type of sealing may be necessary. Although clay soils are good for holding water, they are not good surface soils for wetlands because they are low in nutrients. For this reason, you may need to import a suitable soil to cover the bare substrate. Six inches to one foot of organic soil is generally desirable.

Hydrology

For a wetland to function, it must have adequate amounts of water during appropriate times of the year. A detailed assessment should be made of the sources and losses of water, and water storage characteristics in the wetland. Sources of water include precipitation, surface runoff, stream flow, springs and seeps, subsurface ground water, and pumped water. Losses of water are due to evapotranspiration, soil infiltration, and wetland outflow. If runoff will primarily supply the water, then the amount of surface runoff for the site must be calculated before determining wetland size. Detailed equations have been developed for determining these hydrologic features. If ground water is to supply the water for the wetland, then the depth to ground water, range of water table fluctuation, and the yield of springs or seepages should be determined. An inexpensive way to monitor ground water with a piezometer is described in Chapter 4.

The hydrologic study should also look at potential maximum extent of flooding, the downstream impact of impounding or diverting water, and water chemistry. Water chemistry is important in determining the types of plants and animals which can live there. When analyzing the potential for flooding and the impacts of impounding or diverting water, it is very important to consider potential impacts to neighboring property owners.

Step 3 - Project Design and Implementation

Based on the results of your project planning, there are many design and implementation strategies available. Some of the most common options to consider are listed below.

Blocking Existing Drainage Systems

One of the most cost-effective wetland restoration activities is to block existing drainage systems by breaking field tiles or blocking drainage ditches. If your project involves a designated drain, it may first be necessary to have the drain officially abandoned. The process for abandoning a drain is in Chapter 17 of the Drain Code.

Dams, Dikes, and Levees

Usually, these are embankments of earth constructed to contain water. They must be properly designed to prevent failure from overtopping, seepage, sloughing, or collapse. Design features include soil engineering properties, positioning, height, side slope, erosion control, and the use of special construction materials (like anti-seep collars on culverts).

Water Control Structures

These are often necessary to control flow to and from the wetland. They include spillways, pipes with drop inlet, pumps, and subsurface drain tiles.

Excavations

On suitable sites, excavated wetlands are the simplest to build, require less engineering, and are safer with respect to possible damage from flooding. However, they are usually restricted to relatively small areas of flat terrain.

Substrate Seals

When soils are too permeable, excessive seepage losses may occur. This may be the result of an inadequate site investigation or a decision that the need for a wetland on a permeable site is more important than site restrictions. In this case, the bottom of the wetland needs to be sealed. Methods of sealing include soil compaction, importing clay soils, adding bentonite (a type of clay which swells when wet) to native soils, or the use of special waterproof linings of plastic or rubber.

Vegetation

A thriving, diverse vegetation community is an important component of a functioning wetland. Vegetation can be established by two primary processes: natural colonization and planting. So long as wetland hydrology is present, some type of wetland vegetation will eventually become established. However, for natural colonization to occur in a timely manner, a source of seeds must be present in the soil or in adjacent wetland vegetation communities. Seed banks of formerly drained areas usually provide excellent sources for wetland vegetation. Wetland restoration projects in these areas generally have a high level of success.

Although rarely necessary, you can establish vegetation by planting seeds, bulbs, root stock, or transplanted sprigs. Transplanting is generally the most successful method (seeding is slower, has a lower survival rate, and is less predictable). Try to use locally grown plants, as they will be better adapted to local environmental conditions. Collecting wild local plants can be environmentally damaging (and illegal in most cases). There are many wetland nurseries which can provide plants, and several guidebooks which describe environmental requirements and general planting guidelines. Newly planted vegetation is subject to being wiped out by hungry populations of wildlife. To ensure that your investment in roots and bulbs does not go to fattening up the local goose or deer population, freshly planted wetland vegetation may need to be protected in some way (e.g., enclosing them in fencing). After a planted vegetation community is established, it will likely change over time due to the dynamic nature of natural communities.

Accessory Structures

These include boardwalks, observation platforms, nesting or loafing structures for wildlife, fencing, access roads, etc.

As mentioned above, it is advisable to seek the expertise of professionals when planning and designing restoration, high impact enhancement, or creation projects. Not only will these individuals provide valuable insight into site assessment and design, but they can also help to secure necessary permits. A permit may be needed when draining, dredging, filling, or other construction or soil disturbance occurs in regulated wetlands or legally established drains. Before commencing a project,

check with the Michigan Department of Environmental Quality, U. S. Army Corps of Engineers, the county drain commissioner, and local governments to determine which permits will be required.

During implementation of the project, design modifications necessary to achieve success may become apparent. Closely inspect the work of contractors to be sure that the design is being followed. Correcting oversights once the land is flooded can be difficult. Special equipment, such as vehicles equipped to work in soft ground or water, may be necessary. Scheduling construction for the driest times of the year may be wise.

Step 4 - Monitoring and Routine Maintenance.

Monitoring is recommended for all wetland restoration, creation, and enhancement projects to measure the success of the project. Most wetlands which have been restored or created are not assessed adequately to determine whether they have been successful. Monitoring and assessment of these areas should continue for at least five years and include: water levels throughout the year, establishment of wetland vegetation, use by animal species, development of wetland soil profiles, and patterns of plant succession. If monitoring indicates that the goals for the project are not being met, then corrective action can be taken.

Minimal maintenance activities are often required to ensure success. Typical maintenance activities include maintaining buffer zones, preventing soil erosion and sedimentation, inspecting and nurturing plantings, and controlling exotic species. In some cases, ongoing operational management is necessary. For instance, seasonal manipulation of the water level in some waterfowl floodings helps to provide maximum food production and nesting habitat.

FUNCTION-BASED PLANNING CONSIDERATIONS

The steps above provide general information regarding the thought process to use when considering a wetland restoration, high-impact enhancement, or creation project. Below are some common planning and design considerations for a variety of wetland functions. It is important to note that these considerations are just a starting point to give you an idea of what activities might be integrated into your plan to address the range of wetland functions. Again, it is recommended that you seek more detailed advice from agency staff, consultants, or your local conservation organization.

Wildlife Habitat

Wetlands provide breeding, nesting, feeding, and safety cover for amphibians, reptiles, birds, and mammals. Wetland restoration and creation projects should be designed to provide habitat elements required for the targeted species of wildlife. Habitat requirements for water, food, cover (for protection from adverse weather and predators), and reproduction (pairing and mating, nesting, brooding) should be considered. The location of the wetland project site in relation to migration corridors as well as proximity to other wetland habitats should also be considered. Species requirements and habitat design elements are detailed in NRCS field office guides, plant and animal reference sheets, and numerous other references.

Fish Habitat

Wetlands provide valuable spawning and nursery areas for fish. They also provide habitat for aquatic invertebrates which are essential for food for fish. If fish habitat is a goal in a creation or enhancement project, then the design must incorporate an area of permanent water. Depending on the desired fish species, it is recommended that some part of the pond be at least eight feet deep to hold fish throughout the year. The bottom topography should be undulating. Parts of the pond designed for breeding and nursery habitat and food production should be less than 3 feet deep and they should have free access to the associated deep water habitats. Water quality, especially summer and winter oxygen levels, is the key to survival and production of fish and other aquatic organisms. Conservation practices are often needed to control watershed erosion and stormwater inputs to ensure that the wetland functions properly.

Water Supply & Ground Water Recharge

Wetlands are a source of ground and surface water. Wetlands store precipitation and runoff for direct or indirect use by humans, livestock, and fish and wildlife. While serving these functions, a wetland can provide habitat for fish, wildlife, and endangered species, and provide recreation and other opportunities. Hydrology is the most critical element of a successful wetland project. Proper design requires a thorough knowledge of the hydrologic inputs and outputs of the system, including infiltration to ground water. If you plan on using the wetland to provide a water supply or to ensure year-round deep water for fish populations, impermeable (or nearly impermeable) substrates are needed. On the other hand, if ground water recharge is a goal, then a somewhat permeable substrate is a necessity.

Habitat for Threatened and Endangered Species

Wetlands provide critical habitat for many federal and state listed threatened and endangered species. Many rare species and species of special concern that may be candidates for listing are also dependent on wetlands. If you are fortunate enough to have threatened or endangered species on your property, you have an exciting opportunity to protect and enjoy a plant or animal that very few other people even get a chance to see. Because their population levels are so low, endan-

gered species require special consideration. Management for threatened or endangered species of plants or animals can often exclude or limit management of wetlands for other uses, even other wildlife resources. On the other hand, management for other functions, such as waterfowl hunting, water storage, and flood control, may be compatible with the needs of endangered species. In regard to planning and design, specific requirements of targeted species of animals or plants must be considered. Recovery Plans developed by the U.S. Fish and Wildlife Service and other information on the species must be referred to for habitat needs and design requirements.

Recreation

Wetlands are used for hunting, trapping, fishing, bird-watching, photography, painting, boating, canoeing, hiking, and for general enjoyment of the beauty of a

natural environment. Recreational activities may be restricted during periods where some species of wildlife are especially sensitive to human disturbance, such as breeding and nesting seasons. Specific requirements for desired experiences and level of activity must be considered in the design phase, as must the type of materials and construction methods, as well as compatibility with other wetland resources. Recreation design can include special features such as access points, walkways, paths, and observation platforms to facilitate enjoyment of the wetland. Keep in mind, however, that permits are needed for construction of boardwalks in regulated wetlands.

Water Quality Maintenance

Natural physical, chemical, and biological processes at work in wetlands help to maintain water quality. It is important to keep two basic considerations in mind when considering designing wetlands to serve this function: wetlands can easily be over stressed by the input of too many pollutants, and wetlands that are used as a treatment area for polluted water can serve as a dangerous "attractive nuisance" for wildlife. Accordingly, design of wetlands for water quality purposes must be based on the concentration of the contaminants in the influent, treatment objectives, and the compatibility with other potential functions. If the primary function of the wetland is to improve water quality, then some sort of pretreatment basin that can be physically cleaned out may be desirable to extend the life of the wetland and allow other functions to operate. Design considerations include detention time, vegetation type(s), soils, and allowances for removal of vegetation and accumulated pollutants. The effectiveness of the wetland in removing the contaminants is increased by spreading the influent evenly over the wetland, having a diversity of vegetation communities, eliminating stagnant areas, and increasing the amount of time water stays in the wetland.

Sediment Control

Reduction of the velocity of water flowing through a wetland due to the physical structures of wetland vegetation and generally flat topography traps sediments. Use of wetlands for sediment control can benefit many other uses through improved water quality downstream. Like with excess contaminants, excess sediment load into a wetland can impair its ability to serve other wetland functions. Design of wetlands for sediment control must consider the quantity and characteristics of the sediment anticipated over the life of the project. If the expected sediment load is so great that it would require periodic removal and proper disposal of sediment, then construction of a sediment basin may be a more appropriate solution to the problem. The best way to deal with sedimentation, however, is to take corrective actions at its source. There are many resources available to help landowners control erosion that may be impacting wetlands or other water resources.

Erosion Control

Wetland vegetation along the Great Lakes, inland lakes, rivers, and streams controls shoreline and streambank erosion through two basic mechanisms: soil stabilization at the land/water interface by roots of vegetation, and by slowing current speed and dampening wave energy. Stabilization of banks and shorelines with wetland vegetation can benefit many other uses, primarily through reduction of sediment and improved water quality. In addition, wetland vegetation installed for erosion control provides habitat for wildlife, improves aesthetic and recreational values, and protects the adjoining uplands from erosion. Because wetland restoration projects to control erosion are usually located in areas that are prone to erosion, they often require careful and vigilant maintenance during establishment.

Flood Storage

Wetlands trap and store water during heavy rainfall and slowly release it to downstream areas, lowering flood peaks and maintaining stream flows during dry periods. Numerous smaller wetlands in a watershed can cumulatively have a significant effect on flood water storage. Flood waters stored in wetlands with more permeable substrates can also benefit ground water recharge. When designing for flood storage, the primary factors to keep in mind are the location of your project in the watershed and the hydrology of the lake or stream system, including average and expected flood elevation and duration. Design of wetlands for flood storage can incorporate many other wetland functions.

Timber Production

With proper management, forest products can be harvested in a way that is compatible with other wetland functions and values. The habitat needs of rare, threatened, and endangered forest species should be carefully considered in planning any harvest or timber management activities. It is important to plant or assure the natural revegetation of several key indigenous cover and food-producing species to encourage and provide habitat diversity. The effect of timber harvesting practices on other wetland functions, the landscape setting, and the needs of the landowner must be carefully considered. In wetlands, intensive timber harvest can impact hydrology and nutrient cycling, expose remaining trees to wind-throw, and be difficult to revegetate. State forestry and wildlife agencies and private forestry consultants can help landowners in the development of timber management plans.

Education and Research

Wetlands are unique ecosystems that provide great outdoor classrooms to teach practically all aspects of ecology and serve as important laboratories for scientific research. Education and research activities are generally compatible with other functions, although human activity may at times impair use by wildlife, particularly for sensitive species during critical times of the year. Specific design criteria may only be needed where special landscape features must be restored or constructed to accommodate educational objectives (e.g., inclusion of deep water habitat for "pond life" exercises). Depending on the intended use of the wetland, the design may also need to consider issues related to accessibility for school groups, etc.

Open Space and Aesthetic Quality

Wetlands can be areas of great diversity and beauty and provide open space for recreational and visual enjoyment. The natural beauty of wetland ecosystems can be readily designed into restored and created wetlands. Although beauty is in the eye of the beholder, designing for aesthetics generally includes the establishment of a diversity of vegetation communities, planting native flowering herbs or shrubs in highly visible areas, and allowing for a combination of near and far vistas when possible. Care must be taken to assure that any boardwalks or observation platforms blend in with the surroundings.

SUMMARY

Private landowners present the greatest opportunity to improve Michigan's wetland resources through wetland restoration, enhancement, and creation activities. This chapter provides you with the basic steps to successfully plan and implement a restoration and creation project, and brief descriptions of the considerations that must be made if you are thinking about designing for specific wetland functions. Some wetland restoration and enhancement projects are fairly straightforward, while others are considerably more complex. If you think you have a former wetland on your property that you would like to restore, or if there is an area on your property where you would like to create a wetland, it is recommended that you contact one of the many organizations and agencies listed in Chapter 10 and the appendices that assist landowners in planning, design, and implementation of wetland restoration, enhancement, and creation projects.

Regulatory Requirements

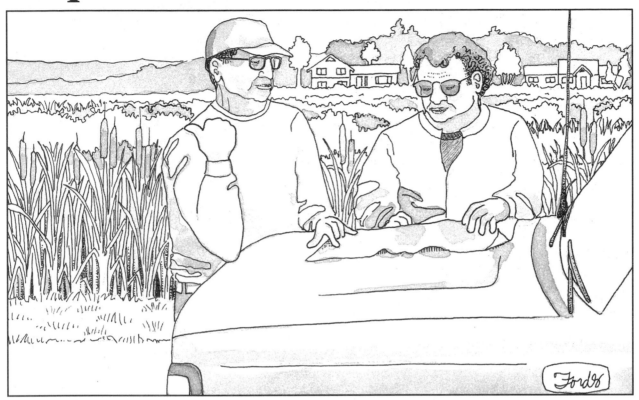

When considering options for wetland conservation and management, or development or construction in and around wetlands, landowners need to be aware of federal, state, and local regulatory requirements. Laws that regulate activities in wetlands have proven to be some of our most controversial environmental protection statutes. In response to this controversy, each year there are attempts at federal and state levels to modify wetland laws and regulations. As such, there is the ever present potential that laws and regulations may change. Regardless of this potential, it is essential that landowners have the best information available about wetland laws so that they may realize their legal rights and responsibilities. The information contained in this chapter provides the most accurate and up-to-date information available at the time of publication. To ensure accuracy regarding wetland regulations in Michigan, it may be necessary to contact one of the resource agencies listed in the appendices.

THE BASIS FOR WETLAND REGULATIONS

As noted in Chapter 2, wetlands provide many important functions that benefit not only the landowner, but others as well. The value of these wetland benefits to society is typically referred to as the public interest. The purpose of wetland regulation is to explicitly acknowledge the public interest in wetland protection and provide guidelines for activities in wetlands that protect the public interest.

Given that a landowner has certain rights that run with the title of a piece of property, wetland laws attempt to navigate the sometimes rocky waters of determining where an individual's property rights end and where the public's interest in resource protection begins. An analogy that is sometimes helpful is the example of the fist and the nose: my individual "right" to swing my fist is restricted by my responsibility to respect your nose. In the terms of wetland regulation, my right as a property owner to alter my wetland (dredge, fill, drain, etc.) is limited by my

responsibility to act in a way that does not adversely impact you or society at large. Of course, there are situations when it is legally and morally acceptable for my fist to connect with someone's nose (e.g., self defense). Likewise, there are situations in which activities regulated by wetland laws are permitted to occur (e.g., when all less damaging alternatives have been utilized and impacts have been mitigated).

In short, because wetlands function in a way that benefits the public, landowners have a responsibility to act in a way that does not unnecessarily adversely impact the public interest in those benefits.

MICHIGAN'S WETLAND REGULATORY PROGRAM

At the heart of Michigan's wetland regulatory program is Part 303, Wetland Protection, of the Natural Resources and Environmental Protection Act (Act 451 of 1994), formerly referred to as the Goemaere-Anderson Wetlands Protection Act, P.A. 203 of 1979 (see appendices for full text). The MDEQ Land and Water Management Division administers the permit program. As part of this program, the MDEQ has assumed the administration of Section 404 of the Clean Water Act (see discussion later in this chapter).

Michigan's Wetland Protection Act has several components. First, it establishes a state policy to protect the public against the loss of wetlands and makes explicit findings as to the benefits wetlands provide. Second, it establishes a permit program regulating some activities in wetlands which are above the ordinary high water mark of lakes and streams. Third, the Wetland Protection Act provides enforcement language and sets maximum penalties for violations. Fourth, it explicitly authorizes regulation of wetlands by local governments.

Activities Regulated

Under Michigan's Wetland Protection Act, a permit is required for the following activities:

1) Deposit or permit the placing of fill material in a wetland;
2) Dredge, remove, or permit removal of soil or minerals from a wetland;
3) Construct, operate, or maintain any use or development in a wetland; or
4) Drain surface water from a wetland.

It is important to note that these activities are regulated regardless of the intention of the dredging, filling, construction, or draining activities. For example, if a landowner plans to fill a wetland to construct a dike for the purpose of a waterfowl flooding, this activity still requires a permit even though the landowner may feel that the project will benefit the environment.

Definition

The activities that are regulated by the Wetland Protection Act only apply to wetlands as defined in the Act. The definition of wetlands in the Act has two components. First, the Act defines wetland as "land characterized by the presence of water at a frequency and duration sufficient to support, and that under normal circumstances does support, wetland vegetation or aquatic life, and is commonly referred to as a bog, swamp, or marsh." Chapter 3 provides details on how this definition is actually implemented to make wetland determinations and delineate wetland boundaries.

Second, jurisdiction over wetlands depends on whether a wetland is contiguous to a water body. Contiguous wetlands are those found in close proximity to a lake, stream, pond, Great Lake, etc., and/or have a direct hydrological relationship with it. According to the administrative rules promulgated for the Act (see appendices), wetlands within 500 feet of an inland lake, stream, or pond and within 1,000 feet of a Great Lake generally are considered contiguous. Noncontiguous wetlands are isolated from lakes and streams hydrologically and, generally, geographically.

Activities in contiguous wetlands are regulated without regard to the size of the wetland because of their close relationship to lakes and streams. Noncontiguous wetlands, however, are regulated only if they are greater than five acres in size. In counties of less than 100,000 people, noncontiguous wetlands are not usually regulated until a wetland inventory is complete. The MDEQ can regulate noncontiguous wetlands of any size anywhere in the state if the wetland is determined to be essential to the preservation of natural resources of the state and the landowner is notified of this determination.

Exemptions

A variety of activities are exempt from wetland regulations, including recreational activities, vegetation clearing, and nearly all agricultural activities. Specific exemptions are listed in Section 30305 of the Act (see appendices) but are still subject to other laws of the state. If you are unclear whether an activity is exempt, contact the MDEQ Land and Water Management Division.

General Permits

The MDEQ may issue general permits on a state or county basis for a category of activities that are similar in nature and have only a minimal adverse individual or cumulative effect on the environment. In the current program, applications under a general permit still undergo a full review, including a site inspection or the review of site specific information, and must meet all regulatory standards. However, the general permit process allows the Department to reach a decision without public notice. This allows the MDEQ to process minor applications more quickly. The Department has the option to issue a public notice on an application that would otherwise qualify under a general permit category if they determine that the project warrants public review and comment.

Permit Standards

Section 30311 of the Wetland Protection Act details the specific standards that must be met before a permit is issued. If you are considering applying for a wetland permit, you should familiarize yourself with the specific permit review standards. The permit standards essentially involve the application of three "tests" to each application: public interest, acceptable disruption to aquatic resources, and wetland dependency/alternatives analysis.

Public Interest Test

The rationale behind wetland regulation is that the public interest in the functions that wetlands provide is in need of protection. Accordingly, the regulatory agency responsible for making wetland permit decisions must determine the impact of the project on the public interest. In determining whether the proposed activity is in the public interest, the reasonably foreseeable benefits of the project are weighed against the reasonably foreseeable detriments. Since wetland dredging, filling, and draining typically benefit the applicant, whereas the detriments are typically felt by the public at large, the public interest test usually boils down to the hard question of private gain versus public loss. To help agency staff negotiate the public interest test, Michigan's wetland protection law provides a list of nine issues to consider, ranging from the cumulative impacts of existing and future activities in the watershed to the public and private economic value of the proposed land change in the general area.

Acceptable Disruption to Aquatic Resources Test

According to Section 30311(4) of the Act, "a permit shall not be issued unless it is shown that an unacceptable disruption will not result to the aquatic resource."

In applying this test, the law instructs agency staff to consider all the functions and values that wetlands provide, including flood storage, fish and wildlife habitat, erosion control, and the range of water quality protection functions.

Wetland Dependency/ Alternatives Analysis Test

Section 30311(4) also states that "a permit shall not be issued" unless the applicant shows either that the proposed activity is "primarily dependent upon being located in the wetland" or that " a feasible and prudent alternative does not exist." The rationale behind this test is simple: if there is a way to accomplish the goals of the project in a way that damages the wetland less, then it should be taken.

These two components are linked because the result of the first part (wetland dependency) impacts the rigor of the alternatives analysis. If a project is determined to be wetland dependent (e.g. peat mining, since peat only forms in wetlands), then the alternatives to accomplish the goals of the project are limited. However, if the project is not wetland dependent (e.g., constructing a home), then less damaging alternatives are presumed to exist. It is the task of the applicant to provide information to counter this presumption. The overall goal of this test is to first avoid impacts to wetlands, then to minimize those that are not avoidable. Mitigation is usually required to offset unavoidable impacts.

These three tests serve as the justification for permit denial or approval. If you plan on applying for a permit, a thorough understanding of the specific language contained in the law will help to ensure that you understand the statutory obligations of the agency staff charged with administering it.

Michigan's wetland protection statute authorizes the MDEQ to require mitigation for unavoidable adverse impacts that otherwise meet the permit criteria described above. The mitigation guidelines listed in the administrative rules seek no net loss of wetlands and mitigation projects that will replace the lost wetland functions on or near the same site as the impacted wetland. If that is determined to not be possible or beneficial to the resource, then a high priority is placed on requiring mitigation within the same watershed.

Application Procedures

Application for a wetland permit is made to the Land and Water Management Division of the Michigan Department of Environmental Quality (MDEQ). The

Land and Water Management Division also administers other laws that regulate activities in and around the land-water interface (briefly described later in this chapter). In situations where two or more resource management acts apply, the Land and Water Management Division reviews one permit application under the criteria of all the applicable acts. For example, activities in wetlands requiring a permit under Inland Waters (Part 301 of Act 451 of 1994) and the Wetland Protection statute require only one permit application. This permit consolidation prevents unnecessary duplication of permits and review processes.

The process for applying for a permit is fairly simple: get the application, fill it out completely, submit it to the resource agency, and be available to discuss the specifics of the project. However, many landowners find the process to be frustrating. Much of the frustration can be reduced by hiring a consultant to complete the application materials and serve as your agent in dealing with the MDEQ staff. If you would rather go through the process yourself, you can reduce your frustration by comprehensively planning the project and becoming knowledgeable about the specific criteria that your application will be judged against. To help you do this, the entire text of the Wetland Protection part of Act 451 is included in this guidebook. One way to assist you with planning your project and completing your application might be to place yourself in the shoes of the person who will be making the permit decision and asking the questions he or she must ask: Is this project in the public interest? Are the disruptions to aquatic habitats acceptable? Have I utilized all alternatives that would accomplish the goal of the project while avoiding or minimizing impacts to the wetlands? If you can develop your project in a way that allows you to answer yes to all these questions, then your experience with the wetland regulatory process should be relatively painless.

Once an application is submitted to the MDEQ in Lansing, the Permit Consolidation Unit (PCU) staff will determine if the application is complete. If some materials are missing or information is unclear, the PCU staff will contact you either by phone or in writing. After the determination is made that all information has been provided and the application is complete, the clock on the 90-day time limit imposed by the law for the MDEQ to process the application starts ticking. Depending on the nature of the project, the MDEQ staff may issue a public notice. Any comments from the public regarding your project must be considered in your permit review, including requests for a public hearing. If a public hearing is held on your project, you will want to prepare a presentation to be made to the public to explain your project and answer any questions that might be raised. It is important to note that if a public hearing is held, the MDEQ has 90 days after the conclusion of the hearing to make a decision. After the MDEQ staff member has gathered relevant information and considered public comments, he or she makes a decision as to whether to issue or deny the permit, or issue the permit with modifications. If you receive a permit denial and would like to contest the decision, you have the opportunity to file a petition for administrative appeal.

Enforcement

Wetland property owners should be aware of the stiff penalties that come with violating Michigan's wetlands law. Failure to obtain a necessary permit, or violations of permit conditions, are subject to civil and criminal penalties. Actions may be brought by either local prosecutors or by Michigan's Attorney General. If found to be in violation, financial penalties, restoration, and/or jail sentences may be imposed by court verdict or order. The court may impose a civil fine of $10,000 per day of violation of the law or violation of a court order, as well as ordering wetland restoration.

Criminal penalties are slightly different. A person who violates the Act is punishable by a fine of up to $2,500. Willful or reckless violations of permit

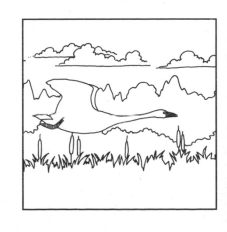

conditions by a person or corporate officer can result in a fine of not less than $2,500 nor more than $25,000 per day of violation, and/or imprisonment for not more than one year. A second such violation constitutes a felony, punishable by a fine of up to $50,000 per day of violation, and/or up to two years of imprisonment. In addition to these penalties, the court may order a person who violates this act to restore the affected wetland.

Other State Laws Affecting Wetlands

The role of state government in protecting Michigan's Natural Resources is mandated by the Michigan Constitution of 1963. Article 4, Section 53 of the Constitution provides that:

> The conservation and development of the natural resources of the state are hereby declared to be of paramount public concern in the interest of the health, safety and general welfare of the people. The legislature shall provide for the protection of the air, water, and other natural resources of the state from pollution, impairment and destruction.

Consistent with this mandate, there are many state regulations that affect wetlands in Michigan. A brief synopsis of these laws appears below.

Soil Erosion and Sedimentation Control (Part 91 of Act 451 of 1994, formerly P.A. 347 of 1972) is designed to protect the waters of the state from sedimentation caused by soil erosion. Permits are required for earth changes which disturb one or more acres of land or which are within 500 feet of a lake or stream, excluding plowing, tilling, mining, and logging land uses. Before a permit is issued, the applicant must prepare a soil erosion and sedimentation control plan. Permits are issued by counties or local agencies through programs approved by the MDEQ.

Subdivision Control (P.A. 288 of 1968) requires the approval of the Michigan Department of Environmental Quality for the preliminary plat of any subdivision containing lots within or affected by a floodplain, and any subdivision involving land abutting a lake or stream where public rights may be affected. In many cases, wetlands are involved and are brought to the attention of the appropriate agencies during the review process.

Michigan Environmental Protection Act (MEPA) (Part 17 of Act 451 of 1994, formerly P.A. 127 of 1970) places a duty on all individuals and organizations, whether private or public, to prevent or minimize environmental degradation which is caused or likely to be caused by their activities. Its requirements are in addition to those provided by any other law. MEPA prohibits any conduct which is likely to pollute, impair, or destroy a lake, stream, wetland, or other natural resource of the state unless the entity proposing or authorizing the activity can show: 1) there are no less harmful feasible and prudent alternatives; and 2) the "conduct is consistent with the promotion of the public health, safety and welfare in light of the state's paramount concern for the protection of its natural resources from pollution, impairment or destruction." Any person, organization, or governmental body can go to court to enforce MEPA against any other person, organization, or governmental body.

Michigan Endangered Species (Part 365 of Act 451 of 1994, formerly P.A. 203 of 1974) requires a permit for activities that could adversely impact threatened and endangered plant and animal species or their habitat. Since a large percentage of Michigan's endangered or threatened species reside in wetland areas, this law is often involved with wetland projects.

Water Resources Protection (Part 31 of Act 451 of 1994, formerly P.A. 167 of 1968) assesses the location and extent of floodplains, streambeds, stream discharge, and stage characteristics for the state's watercourses to minimize flood damage. A permit is required for any dredging, grading, or construction of a building within the 100-year floodplain of any river, stream, or lake.

Inland Waters (Part 301 of Act 451 of 1994, formerly P.A. 346 of 1972) regulates activities in lakes and streams and associated wetlands, excluding the Great Lakes and Lake St. Clair. The Act applies to artificial or natural lakes, rivers, streams, and creeks as defined by having definite banks, a bed, and visible evidence of a continued flow or continued occurrence of water. This includes intermittent or seasonal streams. Permits are required to dredge, fill, or construct or place structures below the ordinary high water mark and connect any waterway to an inland lake or stream.

Shorelands Protection and Management (Part 323 of Act 451 of 1994, formerly P.A. 245 of 1970) protects parts of the Great Lakes shoreline that are specifically designated by the Natural Resources Commission as high risk erosion, flood risk, and environmental areas. To be designated, environmental areas must be deemed necessary for the preservation and maintenance of fish and wildlife along shorelines of the Great Lakes, including those areas influenced by Great Lakes water level fluctuations.

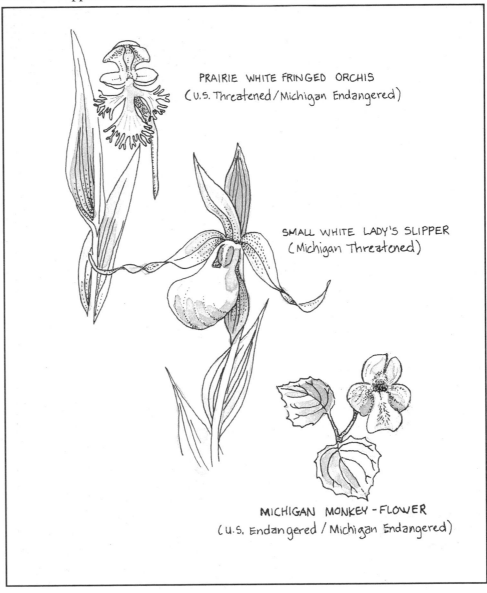

PRAIRIE WHITE FRINGED ORCHIS
(U.S. Threatened / Michigan Endangered)

SMALL WHITE LADY'S SLIPPER
(Michigan Threatened)

MICHIGAN MONKEY-FLOWER
(U.S. Endangered / Michigan Endangered)

Sand Dunes Protection and Management (Part 353 of Act 451 of 1994, formerly P.A. 146 and P.A. 147 of 1989) regulates activities in designated critical dune areas in Michigan, many of which contain interdunal wetland swales. The Act regulates construction activities, vegetation removal, and other uses involving contour change that may increase erosion and decrease stability.

Common Law

It is possible that an alteration of a watercourse or wetland may alter streamflow, water quality, or runoff patterns so that certain common law doctrines may be relevant. Riparian, surface water, nuisance, and trespass laws may all apply. For instance, if an adjacent landowner alters surface water flows so as to discharge an increased amount of water into your wetland, you could file suit for damages and an injunction preventing further discharge in excess of natural conditions.

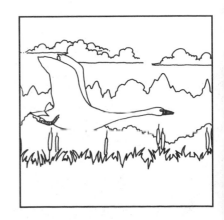

THE FEDERAL WETLAND REGULATORY PROGRAM

The federal government's power to regulate discharges into the waters of the United States arises from authority conferred on Congress by the "Commerce Clause" contained in the U.S. Constitution. The phrase "waters of the United States" is broadly defined to include rivers, lakes, streams, ponds, and wetlands that are, or could be, used in interstate commerce. Since this criteria can be met if a particular wetland supports recreation activities, supports a commercial fishery, or provides habitat for any one of the more than 800 federally listed migratory birds, practically

all wetlands in the country are considered "waters of the United States."

The U.S. Environmental Protection Agency (EPA) is ultimately responsible for the administration of the Clean Water Act. In Michigan, the MDEQ and the U.S. Army Corps of Engineers (Corps) share the responsibility of administering and enforcing the federal wetlands regulatory program with oversight by the EPA. The wetland regulatory authority and responsibilities of the Corps are based on Section 10 of the Rivers and Harbors Act of 1899 (33 U.S.C. 403) and Section 404 of the Clean Water Act of 1977 (33 U.S.C. 1344). The Corps has the authority to bring enforcement actions, including criminal or civil actions, against violators of these laws. In addition, the EPA also has authority to enforce Section 404.

Section 10 of the Rivers and Harbors Act of 1899

Section 10 of the Rivers and Harbors Act of 1899 (33 U.S.C. 403) regulates virtually all work in, over, and under waters listed as "navigable waters of the United States." Some typical examples of projects requiring Section 10 permits include beach nourishment, boat ramps, breakwaters, bulkheads, dredging, filling, or discharging material (such as sand, gravel, or stone), groins and jetties, mooring buoys, piers (seasonal or permanent), placement of rock riprap for wave protection or streambank stabilization, boat hoists, pilings, and construction of marina facilities. Section 10 waters include the Great Lakes, connecting waters, and those inland waters that have been designated as federally navigable (e.g., Lake Charlevoix, parts of St. Joseph River, etc.)

Section 404 of the Clean Water Act

The Section 404 program—the primary federal program governing activities in wetlands—regulates the discharge of dredged or fill material into the waters of the United States (the definition of which includes wetlands) and is intended to minimize adverse impacts by preventing the unnecessary loss of wetlands and other sensitive aquatic areas. Filling and grading, mechanized land clearing, ditching or other excavation activity, property protection devices such as rock riprap, seawalls, groins, and breakwaters, and piling installation all constitute discharges of dredged and/or fill material under the Corps' regulatory authority.

State Assumption and Administration of Section 404

The MDEQ (formerly the MDNR) assumed administration of the Section 404 wetlands program in 1984. Authority to assume the program was granted due to the similarities between Section 404 and the activities regulated by Michigan's regulations affecting wetlands, and because MDEQ had demonstrated its ability to administer the regulations as effectively as federal agencies. Primary oversight responsibility for a state-assumed permit program rests with the EPA. EPA's authority allows it to review all Section 404 permit applications submitted to the state. However, the EPA has waived review of all applications except "major discharges." "Major discharges" are defined, in part, as:

1) Greater than 10,000 cubic yards of fill;
2) Discharges that contain toxic materials; and
3) Discharges into areas determined to be unique, or where the waterway's commercial value could be significantly reduced.

In the case of "major discharge" applications, the EPA coordinates review of the application by the Corps and the U.S. Fish and Wildlife Service through the public notice process. Although the state still has jurisdiction, the MDEQ cannot issue a Section 404 permit over an objection from the EPA. If the state and the EPA disagree, and EPA's objections cannot be resolved, then 404 jurisdiction for that particular application reverts to the Corps.

In addition to this arrangement, the Corps has retained jurisdiction over the Section 10 activities as described above and Section 404 activities in Great Lakes coastal areas, their connecting waterways, and major tributaries to the upstream limit of federal navigability. In the areas where the Corps has retained jurisdiction, both a Corps and a MDEQ permit are required for activities in wetlands. For example, in Emmet and Cheboygan Counties along the Inland Water Route, or in the Detroit River, those wishing to alter wetlands must have two permits, one from the MDEQ under the Wetlands Protection Section of Act 451 and one from the Corps under Section 404 and/or Section 10. On the majority of inland wetlands, only a MDEQ permit is required.

For those applying for permits to alter wetlands in joint jurisdictional areas, the MDEQ and the Corps have coordinated efforts to avoid permit duplication. The Corps and the MDEQ have jointly developed a single application form to be completed by the applicant. This one form is sent to the Permit Consolidation Unit of the MDEQ Land and Water Management Division. If the activity requires Corps review, a copy is made and forwarded to the Corps. From this point on, the applications undergo similar, but separate processes. In some cases, an MDEQ permit will be issued, but a Corps permit will be denied, or vice versa. Again, activities in joint jurisdictional waters must have both permits to be authorized. It is important to note that the vast majority of wetlands in the state are not in joint-jurisdictional waters and only a permit from the MDEQ is required.

Corps Administration of Section 404

In the permit review process, the Corps analyzes the impacts of the proposed activity under a simultaneous review process demanded by three different sets of regulations: Regulatory Programs of the Corps (33 CFR Part 320-330), Corps Regulations for Implementing the National Environmental Policy Act (33 CFR Part 23), and, in 404 discharges, the Section 404(b)(1) Guidelines for the Specification of Disposal Sites for Dredged or Fill Material (40 CFR Part 230).

Like Michigan's wetland protection law, the federal wetlands permitting program requires application of a "public interest test." In determining the public interest, the Corps considers all factors of the proposed activity, including conservation, economics, aesthetics, general environmental concerns, historic values, fish and wildlife values, flood damage prevention, land use, navigation, recreation, water supply and water quality, energy needs, safety, food production, and the needs and welfare of the public.

For activities involving 404 discharges, a permit will be denied if the discharge that would be authorized by such a permit would not comply with the U.S. Environmental Protection Agency's 404(b)(1) guidelines. The Corps must prepare an environmental impact assessment and make a finding of whether an environmental impact statement should be prepared. The guidelines require that practicable alternatives to degrading a wetland be considered before a permit is approved. If the basic activity to be carried out on the filled area does not require a wetland in order to take place, it is presumed that practicable alternatives are available. This is the "water dependency test." For example, consider a proposed parking lot in a wetland; parking cars per se does not require the use of a wetland.

The Guidelines also state that no permit should be issued if it would:
1) Cause violations of state water quality standards;
2) Violate toxic effluent standards;
3) Jeopardize federally listed endangered or threatened species;
4) Cause significant adverse effects on municipal water supplies, plankton, fish, shellfish, wildlife, or special aquatic sites (e.g., wetlands);
5) Cause significant adverse effects on the capacity of a wetland to assimilate nutrients, purify water, or reduce wave energy; or
6) Significantly reduce recreational, aesthetic, and economic values.

Mitigation is an important element of both the Section 404(b)(1) guidelines and the public interest review. The term mitigation is defined as the lessening of adverse impacts through avoidance, minimization, and compensation. After strict applications of the permitting standards, a permit may be issued for a project that will have adverse wetland impacts, provided that appropriate and practicable steps are taken to minimize adverse impacts to the aquatic ecosystem and that unavoidable wetland losses are appropriately mitigated.

The Role of Other Agencies

As mentioned above, the U.S. Environmental Protection Agency has ultimate authority over the Section 404 program. The EPA has primary responsibility for approval of 404 regulations, provides comments on water quality issues, ensures compliance with 404(b)(1) guidelines, and has the power to veto some categories of Corps and MDEQ permit decisions. The U.S. Fish and Wildlife Service is charged with reviewing permit applications to assure that impacts on wildlife and endangered species are minimal according to the Fish and Wildlife Act of 1956 (16 U.S.C. 742a, et seq.), the Migratory Marine Game-Fish Act (16 U.S.C. 760c-760g), the Fish and Wildlife Coordination Act (16 U.S.C. 661-666c) and the Endangered Species Act (16 U.S.C. 1531 et seq.).

The Conservation Provisions of the Farm Bill

The Food Security Act (Farm Bill) of 1985, as amended, requires that landowners who receive U.S. Department of Agriculture (USDA) program benefits comply with wetland and highly erodible land requirements. Any person who plants an agricultural commodity on a wetland that was converted after December 23, 1985, or converts a wetland after November 28, 1990, is ineligible for USDA program benefits. Farmers who plant agricultural commodities on highly erodible land must do so according to an approved conservation plan.

LOCAL WETLAND REGULATIONS

In Michigan, local government has traditionally been delegated the primary responsibility to make land use decisions through zoning. Local wetlands protection in addition to MDEQ regulation is consistent with this tradition of " home rule." The Wetland Protection Act authorizes municipalities to regulate wetlands using the same wetland definition, regulatory standards, and application process. This authority is supplemental to the existing authority of a municipality to enact zoning ordinances in the public interest under the County, Township, and City and Village Zoning Enabling Acts. Given the importance of the functions and values that wetlands provide, some municipalities in Michigan have adopted local wetland ordinances.

Local wetland protection can take many forms. Some communities integrate wetland protection provisions into their zoning ordinances, while others have comprehensive stand-alone ordinances with regulatory standards, procedures for permits, and enforcement provisions. Municipalities must also create a wetlands map to accompany the ordinance. The type of wetland protection program enacted in a municipality is based on the level of support for wetland protection, available funding, staff expertise, etc. Accordingly, every local ordinance is different.

Although some wetland property owners may view local wetland ordinances as another layer of regulation, there are many benefits to the applicant that may come from local wetland ordinances. Some of these include:

1) Local wetland inventories developed as part of ordinances can provide the early identification of lands subject to

wetland permits, thus reducing costs and time delays;

2) Local units have the authority to provide incentives for wetland protection that state and federal governments cannot, including cluster options, density bonuses, zoning variances, and tax incentives;

3) Local involvement in wetland regulation helps ensure complete applications and thus expedite and clarify state and federal permit processes; and

4) Local permits can encourage the developer to avoid wetlands early in the development process, thus allowing the applicant to avoid the expensive site engineering that must be done to prepare a wetland site for development.

SUMMARY

Wetland regulations are based on the premise that wetlands provide functions that are valuable to interstate commerce and the public health, safety, and general welfare. Because of the valuable functions that wetlands provide, wetland property owners have a responsibility to act in a way that does not impact the public interest in maintaining wetlands. Wetland laws are designed to balance the public and private interests and direct landowners to a sequence of wetland impact avoidance, minimization, and mitigation. Although there are many "horror stories" of landowners who have had negative experiences in the wetland regulatory process, landowners can reduce their frustrations by proper project planning and appropriately considering the regulatory standards prior to submitting a permit application.

Landowner Assistance: Where to Go for More Help

Because of the many valuable functions that wetlands provide, there are many programs to assist landowners in their efforts to protect, restore, enhance, and create wetlands. Some provide technical assistance, others provide financial assistance, and many provide both. The programs listed below are most commonly utilized by landowners in Michigan to obtain cost-share and technical assistance for wetland restoration, enhancement, and creation. In addition, the appendices contain lists of agencies and organizations that provide technical assistance to landowners. If some of the programs below appeal to you, cross reference the coordinating agency with the lists in the appendices and give them a call. In addition, this chapter contains a section on how to select a wetland consultant.

FEDERAL LANDOWNER ASSISTANCE PROGRAMS

In Michigan, federally-funded programs provide valuable assistance to landowners. Many of these programs are administered by district offices of the Natural Resources Conservation Service or other federal agencies. The primary programs that address wetlands are described below. The administering agency is listed in italics below the program name.

Agricultural Conservation Program
Farm Services Agency

The Agricultural Conservation Program (ACP) is administered by the state and county offices of the Farm Services Agency [formerly the Consolidated Farm Services Agency (and before that the Agricultural Stabilization and Conservation Service)] with technical assistance and program guidance provided by the Natural Resources Conservation Service (NRCS), the U.S. Forest Service, the MDNR Forestry Division, and the Michigan State University Extension Service. The ACP encourages voluntary compliance with federal and state requirements for solving

point and nonpoint source pollution on agricultural land. ACP provides 50% to 75% cost-share funds for approved practices providing long term and community-wide conservation benefits. ACP practices that can help fund wetlands and riparian area restoration and enhancement range from permanent vegetative cover to agricultural pollutant reduction.

ACP agreements can be for one year or more, depending on the practice. When entering an agreement, the farmer pays the total cost of establishing the approved conservation practices and is then reimbursed for the government's share of the cost, which may be as much as 75% of total costs for annual agreements. The maximum cost-share limitations for annual conservation plans is $3,500.

Wetland-Related Agricultural Conservation Program Practices

There are many Agricultural Conservation Program Practices that benefit wetlands. The most popular are listed below. It is important to note that not all these practices are presently approved in all Michigan's counties.

SL1	Permanent Vegetative Cover Establishment
WC1	Water Impoundment Reservoirs
WP1	Sediment Retention, Erosion, or Water Control Structures
WP2	Stream Protection
WP6	Constructed Wetland Systems for Agricultural Water Treatment
WP7	Riparian Buffer Strips
WL1	Permanent Wildlife Habitat
WL2	Shallow Water Areas for Wildlife
WQP1	Source Reduction of Agricultural Pollutants

Long-term agreements require the development of a conservation plan by NRCS and approval by the local conservation district and the FSA county office. Lump sum payments in excess of $3,500 may be authorized for a long term agreement under certain conditions. Farmers and ranchers may enter into pooling agreements to jointly solve mutual conservation problems. Pooling agreements could be used to restore a wetland covering portions of several properties.

To be eligible, the agricultural producer making an application must own between 10 and 1,000 acres and practices approved for cost-sharing must result in long term and community-wide benefits. The practices should also be those that the farmer or rancher would not, or could not, undertake without financial and technical assistance. Applications must be approved by the FSA County Committee.

Conservation Reserve Program
Farm Services Agency

The Conservation Reserve Program (CRP) is one of the primary conversation programs in the Federal Farm Bill (the Food Security Act of 1985, and as amended by the Food, Agriculture, Conservation, and Trade Act of 1990). This program provides an incentive to encourage farmers to enroll highly erodible cropland and/or land contributing to a serious water quality problem into the reserve for 10 to 15 years. In return, farmers receive annual rental payments for the land, cost-sharing, and technical assistance to plant vegetation for conservation. The major goals of CRP include reducing soil erosion and sedimentation, improving water quality, maintaining fish and wildlife habitat, and providing support income to farmers. The program is administered by the FSA in cooperation with the NRCS, Cooperative Extension Service, MDNR Forestry Division, and county soil and water conservation districts.

Although most CRP lands are classed as "highly erodible," fields often include areas of former wetlands that could be restored. Although CRP funds are no longer available to help restore wetlands on these lands, the landowner may do so at anytime. Non-USDA funds can be used to assist in the restoration, as long as the plans for the restoration are included in the landowner's conservation plan maintained by the U.S. Natural Resources Conservation Service.

Wetlands Reserve Program
Natural Resources Conservation Service

The Wetlands Reserve Program (WRP) is another important conservation component of the Farm Bill and was authorized by the Food, Agriculture, Conservation, and Trade Act of 1990. WRP is a voluntary program offering landowners a

chance to receive payments for restoring wetlands. Under WRP, landowners are provided cost-share funds to restore wetlands in return for a conservation easement. Areas under easement can also include existing natural wetlands and adjacent uplands deemed necessary to protect the wetlands.

Owners of eligible lands apply for enrollment at their local NRCS or USDA Farm Services Office by declaring their intent to participate during the specified enrollment periods. The NRCS and the U.S. Fish and Wildlife Service (FWS) then determine the eligibility of the acres offered. Sites are ranked using a variety of priority factors, including: 1) habitat for migratory birds and other wildlife; 2) wetland functions; 3) location significance; 4) wetland management requirements; and 5) physical conditions of the site.

A Wetland Reserve Plan of Operations (WRPO) is developed for each of the high priority areas. The NRCS, with the assistance of FWS, will help landowners develop the plans. Each plan will describe intentions and objectives as to restoration practices needed to accomplish the restoration, landowner requirements for maintaining the restored wetland values, and other details. The acceptable uses of the land after the easement is filed will also be spelled out in detail in the WRPO.

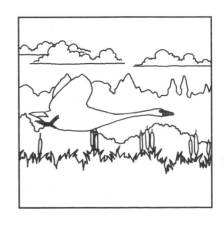

No activities may degrade or diminish the wetland functions and values of the land under easement.

After completion and approval of the plan by the agencies and the landowner, the landowner may accept the amount offered by NRCS for the easement. The government's offer will be based on the appraised agricultural value of the land. Between 50-100% cost-share will be paid for restoring the wetlands and adjacent lands. All legal costs associated with recording the easement will also be paid by the government.

The landowners will maintain full control over public access to and use of the WRP easement lands. The WRP easement does not open the areas to public hunting, fishing, or other forms of recreation unless the landowner desires to do so. The landowner will be responsible for maintaining the area and for paying property taxes. As with other conservation easements, the reduction in development potential should reduce the property tax burden. Remember, it is the landowner's responsibility to request the post-easement tax assessment from their local tax assessor. When lands are sold, the easement follows the sale and the new owner assumes the easement obligations.

In Michigan, eligible counties are those that occur in the southern half of the lower peninsula.

Debt Cancellation Conservation Easements
Farm Service Agency

Persons with USDA loans secured by real estate may qualify for cancellation of a portion of their debt in exchange for a conservation easement. Originally administered by the former Farmer's Home Administration, this program is now administered by the Farm Service Agency. Easements may be established on wetlands, marginal cropland, and other environmentally sensitive lands for conservation, recreation, and wildlife purposes (See FmHA Program Aid 1528, Debt Cancellation Conservation Easements). Although this program is available throughout the state, it has been used by landowners in very few instances. Like when establishing conservation easements with a private organization, property offered for an easement must meet eligibility and desirability requirements.

By participating in the Conservation Easement Debt Cancellation Program, borrowers reduce their USDA debt, thereby improving their overall financial stability. Also, borrowers can conserve wildlife habitat and improve the environmental and scenic value of their farms. As with other conservation easements, once a conservation easement is established, the property is subject to the easement for its duration, regardless of who owns the land. New owners of the property will be subject to the same restrictions and retain the same rights as the borrower who originally granted the easement in exchange for the USDA debt reduction.

North American Wetlands Conservation Act
U.S. Fish and Wildlife Service
MDNR Wildlife Division

The North American Wetlands Conservation Act (NAWCA) encourages partnerships among public agencies and other interests to: 1) protect, enhance, restore, and manage an appropriate distribution and diversity of wetland ecosystems and other habitats for migratory birds, fish, and wildlife in North America; 2) maintain current or improve distribution of migratory bird populations; and 3) sustain an abundance of waterfowl and other migratory birds consistent with the goals of the North American Waterfowl Management Plan and international treaty obligations.

The Act provides funding for wetland conservation projects involving acquisition, restoration, and/or enhancement. Funding is provided through a competitive grants process by the North American Wetlands Conservation Council (Council) based on recommendations from the Migratory Bird Conservation Commission (MBCC). The U.S. Fish and Wildlife Service (FWS) coordinates with the Council on the NAWCA and can provide assistance to landowners to develop proposals for submission to the Council and MBCC.

Proposals may be submitted by any group or individual by the first Friday in August for funding available October 1st. A proposal must describe how the proposed work fits into a larger project (if applicable); the need for the proposal; where the work is to be done; the effect of the proposal on animals, plants and wetland functions; how much the proposal will cost; and partner commitments and responsibilities. NAWCA grants require a minimum one-to-one grant match from any non-federal source, such as a state, nonprofit group, or landowner. A grant application instruction booklet outlining the above information in more detail is available through the FWS Regional Office in Minneapolis, Minnesota.

North American Waterfowl Management Plan Joint Venture Projects
U.S. Fish and Wildlife Service
MDNR Wildlife Division

The North American Waterfowl Management Plan (NAWMP) is an agreement signed between the United States, Canada, and Mexico to restore waterfowl and other migratory bird populations to levels of the early 1970's by protecting and restoring priority wetland habitats. The plan is implemented through unique partnerships called joint ventures.

The U.S. Fish and Wildlife Service coordinates joint ventures with federal, state, and private agencies, and private individuals that cooperate and pool resources together, including funding, to achieve objectives of the plan. Private landowners of wetlands significant to waterfowl may receive technical and financial assistance through the variety of cooperative programs undertaken within their geographic area. Landowners (federal, state, group, or individual) with property having significant importance to waterfowl and other wetland-dependent species may be eligible for funding under this program.

Partners For Wildlife
U.S. Fish & Wildlife Service

The Partners for Wildlife program offers technical and financial assistance to landowners who wish to restore degraded wetlands, riparian corridors, streams, and other critical habitats. The program focuses primarily on reestablishment of original natural communities. Special consideration is given to projects that contribute to the objectives of the North American Waterfowl Management Plan or the National Wildlife Refuge System, or that contribute to the survival of endangered, threatened, or candidate species, or migratory birds of management concern.

Assistance may take the form of informal advice on the design and location of potential restoration projects, or it may consist of designing and funding restoration projects under a Wildlife Management Agreement with the landowner. Restoration efforts may include, but are not limited to, plugging drainage ditches, installing water control structures, constructing low dikes, fencing riparian corridors, and reestablishing grassland vegetation for nesting cover.

Before funds are spent for project construction, landowners are required to sign a Wildlife Management Agreement through which they agree to leave the habitat restoration project in place for a minimum of 10 years. Longer agreements are desirable, and may be required depending on the cost of the project. Landowners and other partners are encouraged to provide cost-share funds or in-kind services for projects.

Forest Stewardship Program/ Stewardship Incentive Program
MDNR Forestry Division

The Forest Stewardship Program (FSP) and Stewardship Incentive Program (SIP) were established in the 1990 Farm Bill to help landowners protect and enhance their forest lands and associated wetlands. FSP provides technical assistance to help landowners enhance and protect the timber, fish and wildlife habitat, water quality, wetlands, and recreational and aesthetic values of their property. SIP provides cost-share assistance to private landowners for implementing the management plans developed under FSP. Guidelines for SIP define eight major categories for funding: management plan development, reforestation and afforestation, forest and agroforest improvement, windbreak and hedgerow establishment, riparian and wetlands protection and improvement, fisheries habitat enhancement, wildlife enhancement, and forest recreation enhancement.

FSP and SIP are administered by the State Forester in cooperation with the U.S. Forest Service. The Farm Services Agency (FSA) provides administrative assistance. Technical responsibilities for SIP practices may be assigned to various other agencies and resource professionals.

The Forest Stewardship Program (FSP), through state foresters, assists private forest landowners in actively managing their forests and related resources. National program guidelines require wetlands and 11 other resource elements to be considered and evaluated as part of each plan.

The Stewardship Incentive Program provides landowners with financial cost-share assistance to implement completed Forest Stewardship Plans. SIP-6, "Riparian and Wetland Protection and Improvement," is the cost-share practice for restoring and protecting wetlands and riparian areas. Cost share is authorized for purchase, installation and establishment of plant materials, streambank stabilization, fencing, and restoration of natural hydrology.

State forestry staff or qualified private consultants work with private landowners to develop a multiuse Forest Stewardship Resource Conservation Plan specifically for their forested properties. These plans outline a course of action that will enhance forest products, wildlife, soil and water quality, recreation, aesthetics, and environmental quality. Existing management plans can usually be modified to meet Forest Stewardship Plan guidelines. Once a forest management plan has been developed and approved, up to 65 percent of the cost is provided through SIP to fund the plan's projects. Payments to the landowner may not exceed $10,000 per landowner per fiscal year.

Eligible landowners must have an approved Forest Stewardship Plan and own between 12 and 1,000 acres of qualifying land. Authorizations may be obtained for exceptions of up to 5,000 acres. Landowners must maintain and protect SIP funded practices for a minimum of 10 years.

Federal Watershed Management Initiatives
Natural Resources Conservation Service (PL 566)
MDEQ, Surface Water Quality Division (Section 319)
MDEQ, Land and Water Management Division (Section 6217)

There are several federally-funded initiatives that promote watershed management planning activities, including the Watershed Protection and Flood Prevention Program (PL-566), Section 319 of the Clean Water Act (319), and Section 6217 of the Coastal Zone Act Reauthorization Amendments (6217). These programs are designed to provide money to state agencies, Indian tribes, municipalities, or quasi-governmental organizations with authority to carry out, maintain, and operate watershed improvement activities. These programs are most relevant to those landowners who live in watersheds that have received funding under these programs. Landowners in watersheds not funded by these programs may want to consider contacting their county planner, soil and water conservation district staff, or representatives of other eligible agencies to encourage them to prepare a funding proposal.

Under PL-566, the Natural Resources Conservation Service assists state, local, and qualified nonprofit organizations with planning and installing water control and conservation measures in small watershed areas. Projects can be undertaken to restore wetlands and natural stream characteristics throughout a small watershed to improve water quality, wildlife habitat, and general living conditions. Technical assistance, the cost of construction for flood prevention, and cost sharing for other purposes is available. Requests are made through local conservation districts. NRCS assists local sponsors in planning and carrying out measures in authorized project areas. Projects may include wetland protection, flood plain management, and wildlife improvements.

Section 319 of the federal Clean Water Act provides incentives for local units of government to address nonpoint source pollution on a watershed basis. Some activities include:

- Outreach activities to increase awareness of nonpoint source problems and solutions;
- Demonstrations of successful approaches to problems;
- Financial assistance to develop and implement watershed management plans; and
- Improving the scientific foundation for state nonpoint source programs, such as monitoring protocols to evaluate the effectiveness of nonpoint source controls.

Since wetlands serve many functions that improve water quality and abate impacts of nonpoint source pollution, there is a great potential for wetland protection activities to be integrated into Section 319 programs.

Section 6217 of the Coastal Zone Act Reauthorization Amendments of 1990, requires that states with federally-approved coastal zone management programs develop Coastal Nonpoint Pollution Control Programs to be approved by EPA and

NOAA. These programs bring together authorities and capabilities within state coastal zone management and water quality agencies to jointly address the problem of coastal nonpoint pollution. The purpose of the program is to implement specific management measures for controlling nonpoint source pollution by more fully integrating federal, state, and local authorities.

The state Coastal Nonpoint Programs represent an innovative approach to dealing with coastal nonpoint pollution because they build upon state and local authorities and expertise. They employ an initial technology-based approach, generally throughout the coastal management area, followed by a more stringent water quality-based approach to address known water quality problems not solved by the technology-based approach.

STATE LANDOWNER ASSISTANCE PROGRAMS

Several of the federal landowner assistance programs mentioned above are administered by state agencies. In addition to these programs, the Michigan Department of Environmental Quality and Michigan Department of Natural Resources administer the following programs.

Michigan's Farmland and Open Space Preservation Act (PA 116 of 1974)
MDEQ, Land and Water Management Division

Michigan's Farmland and Open Space Preservation Act provides tax relief for landowners who agree to enroll their farmland into the program. Farmland enrolled in P.A. 116 can be farmed, but it cannot be developed in any other way. Essentially, P.A. 116 is a conservation easement program administered by the MDEQ to protect farmland. As in federal farmland set-aside programs, the agreements between the individual and the state are for a minimum 10-year period. As wetlands constitute open space, enrolling them allows an agricultural producer to qualify for tax relief. Farmland can be removed from the program before the agreed-upon period at the request of the owner, with financial penalties.

The fines that have been collected from agricultural producers who have withdrawn from the program early can be used to purchase development rights on farmland. In several instances, these funds have been used to purchase development rights on properties that contained wetlands.

MDNR Nongame Wildlife Fund Grants
MDNR Wildlife Division

The purpose of the Nongame Wildlife Fund Grants is to preserve nongame wildlife species, their habitat, and to increase the public's awareness of these wildlife and plant species. Projects must be compatible with the goals of the Nongame Wildlife Program or specific needs of individual species. Proposals must have a potential to benefit endangered, threatened, or special concern species. Possible activities include surveys, scientific studies, habitat management or protection, and public information and education. No development projects are considered for funding on private land unless they are part of a facility that is open to the public throughout the year.

Individuals, local units of government, educational institutions, and nonprofit organizations are eligible for funding. Grants typically between $200 and $4,000 are awarded. Proposals consistent with nongame wildlife management objectives and with matching funds will receive higher priority.

Local Landowner Assistance Programs
County Soil and Water Conservation Districts

County Soil and Water Conservation Districts coordinate many landowner programs that relate to wetland protection. Conservation Districts are unique local units of government that harness federal, state, and local resources to solve conservation problems. The guiding philosophy of all Conservation Districts is that decisions on conservation problems should be made at the local level, by local people, with technical assistance provided by the government. This philosophy enables them to meet the needs of the communities they serve.

Created to serve as stewards of water and soil resources, Michigan's Conservation Districts take an ecosystem approach to conservation and protection of our resources. Their vision is to help all citizens of their District to have livable communities in harmony with the environment. They have a special role to play in areas where land use change is taking place. Programs carried out by Conservation Districts are as diverse as Michigan's landscape. In southern Michigan, many of the programs deal with the needs of the farm community. In northern Michigan, there is more emphasis on forestry, wildlife, and recreation. Programs of special interest to wetland property owners include watershed management, erosion control, wetland restoration, wildlife habitat management, and tree planting. For more information, contact the Soil and Water Conservation District that serves your county.

NONGOVERNMENTAL ORGANIZATIONS

There are many nonprofit organizations that provide assistance to landowners interested in protecting, restoring, enhancing, or creating wetlands. For example, in northern lower Michigan, the Tip of the Mitt Watershed Council provides technical services such as wetland delineations to landowners. Other organizations, such as the Little Traverse Conservancy, accept donations of land for preservation purposes and assist landowners with placing conservation easements on their property. In addition to the activities mentioned above, several nonprofit organizations in Michigan provide cost-share assistance for landowners interested in restoring and enhancing wetlands. These are briefly described below. See the appendices for numerous additional organizations that provide a variety of services to landowners in every part of Michigan.

Matching Aid to Restore States Habitat (MARSH)
Ducks Unlimited

The MARSH program was instituted in 1985 to develop and protect waterfowl habitat in the United States. This reimbursement program provides matching funds for wetland acquisition and habitat restoration and enhancement in each state based on Ducks Unlimited's (DU's) income within that state.

Projects submitted for MARSH funding must significantly benefit waterfowl. Normally, all projects must be on lands under the control of a public agency or private cooperator with which DU has an approved memorandum of understanding. Control must be through ownership, lease, easement, or management agreement. Control must be adequate for protection, maintenance, and use of the project throughout its projected life.

The amount of money available to fund MARSH projects in each state is currently based on 7.5% of the sum of DU's income within that state, plus any unused money from the previous year. Accordingly, the MARSH allocation will fluctuate as DU's income fluctuates in each state. DU's goal is to match MARSH funds at least dollar for dollar by private, state, or federal sources.

DU will consider proposals from any public or private conservation agency or group that is: 1) able to execute long-term habitat agreements, 2) capable of delivering and managing the projects proposed, and 3) willing to assume all liability associated with the project. In Michigan, the MARSH program is coordinated through the MDNR Wildlife Division. MARSH funds are also used by the U.S. Fish and Wildlife Service Field Office to cost-share wetland restoration projects (see Partners for Wildlife).

Michigan Wildlife Habitat Foundation's Private Wetlands Project
Michigan Wildlife Habitat Foundation

The Michigan Wildlife Habitat Foundation has an innovative wetland restoration program that involves the use of trained volunteers as well as professional staff. Trained volunteers identify potential wildlife restoration areas and help implement wetland restoration projects designed by professionals. The majority of the work involves blocking small open ditches and removing parts of underground drainage tiles to restore wetland hydrology to drained basins.

This program is conducted on private lands only. Landowners must sign an agreement that they will not reverse activities for 10 years. Although the project is focused in the southern half of Michigan's lower peninsula, it is available throughout the state. Michigan Wildlife Habitat Foundation pays for the cost of wetland restoration activity, but requires a minimal cost-share contribution from the landowner. Funds are expended on a first-come, first-served basis.

Pheasants Forever Habitat Grants
Pheasants Forever

Pheasants Forever coordinates a cost-share program to support a variety of habitat enhancement projects that raise the carrying capacity for pheasants and other game and nongame species. Applicable habitat enhancement projects include:

wetland restorations; wetland enhancements to provide more and better wildlife cover; expansion of native warm season grass plantings, food plots, and cool season grass and legume mixtures, especially near wetlands; development of long-term nesting, winter roosting, feeding, and brood rearing pheasant (and other species) habitats on private lands; and development or enhancement of corridors to connect habitat components.

The program operates in counties where present Pheasants Forever chapters exist. Eligible landowners are those that are willing to maintain wetland restoration sites according to federal CRP and WRP guidelines (at least 10 years). Food plots cannot be harvested and nesting covers cannot be mowed before August 1 of each year. Woody covers must remain for a minimum of 10 years. Funding applications should be submitted to Pheasants Forever no later than February 28 for their spring meeting and August 1 for their autumn meeting.

PRIVATE CONSULTANTS

You may find yourself in a situation where the wetland protection, restoration, and enhancement assistance provided by the programs and organizations listed above and in the appendices do not meet your needs. For example, you may want to develop parts of your property and need to know the extent of wetlands and how to avoid and minimize wetland impacts, or you may need assistance in navigating the wetland regulatory process. In this situation, it may be helpful to contact one of the hundreds of private wetland consultants in Michigan who provide these and other services on a fee-for-service basis.

There is an inherent difficulty in finding a qualified consultant since "wetland consultants" are not required to be certified, licensed, or bonded in Michigan. The U.S. Army Corps of Engineers and the Society of Wetland Scientists each have certification programs, and many wetland consultants in Michigan have become certified through these programs. Although no official list of consultant services is available, the Land and Water Management Division of the Michigan Department of Environmental Quality maintains a list of consultants who have submitted their names to the MDEQ. Being included on this list in no way implies endorsement of a consultant's services by the MDEQ. In addition to this list, environmental consultants are sometimes found in the business section of your telephone book, or by asking the advice of individuals or associations who commonly call upon consultants to assist them with wetlands work.

As with any fee-for-service profession, there are a range of skills and expertise that wetland consultants bring with them. Depending on your needs, you may want to select a consultant who can provide more than a wetland delineation and serve as your agent in the permitting process. One of the greatest values that a wetland consultant can add to a project involves their ability to help plan your development to avoid and minimize wetland impacts during and after development of the property. What a consultant knows about site planning and design, stormwater management, landscaping, and management of uplands may be as important as their knowledge of wetlands. The purpose of this section is to provide you with some advice on how you can be a better "consumer" of this service. Wetland consultants charge the same hourly fees that other professionals do (between $75.00 and $200.00). Therefore, you want to make sure you are getting expert service.

Selecting the Right Consultant
Check Credentials

When selecting a wetland consultant, it is important that you carefully evaluate their qualifications, experience, and quality of service. The following suggestions should help you make a reasonable selection.

As you know by reading this book, wetlands are complex ecosystems. Wetland

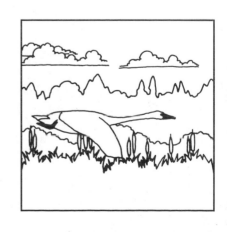

consultants should have a good background in hydrology, soil science, botany, and ecology. In addition, the consultant should be very familiar with local, state, and federal wetland statutes. The consultant should be able to perform wetland delineations in a manner that it consistent with state and federal methods. Specific points to inquire about include years of experience, college course work, professional training, and wetland-related publications.

Check References

Ask the consultant to provide between three and five former wetland clients. Contact these clients to inquire about the quality of service they received. Points to cover include professionalism; working relationship between the consultant, the client, and the regulatory agencies; consistency between the consultant's delineation and the regulatory agency's delineation; cost; and timeliness. In addition, you might want to ask colleagues and other businesses such as real estate, home building, and local environmental organizations typically involved in wetland issues for their impressions of the consultant you are considering.

Examine Workmanship

Ask the wetland consultant to provide you with examples of wetland delineations and permit applications that he or she has completed for other clients. Are the conclusions clear and based on a thorough analysis of hydrology, soils, and vegetation? Is the workmanship and presentation of a high quality? Does the work product appear to be what you want for your project?

By going through this process, you can make your decision on which consultant to select based on solid information. The wetland consultant will benefit from knowing that they have a knowledgeable consumer and a valuable client. You will be sure that you are getting your money's worth.

SUMMARY

There are many programs designed to assist wetland property owners with their efforts to protect, manage, restore, enhance, and create wetlands. This booklet represents a collaborative effort on behalf of dozens of organizations to provide you with information about all aspects of wetland landownership. As stated in the first chapter, wetlands provide a multitude of functions that are valuable to individuals and society at large. For this reason, wetland landowners have a greater responsibility to be good stewards of their property for the benefit of us all. Through proper stewardship, wetland landowners can lead Michigan into the next century by serving as positive role models of how to live with nature's bounty. Living with Michigan's wetlands means that the landowner will be able to experience the beauty and productivity of wetlands firsthand: the mystery of a dark cedar swamp, the chorus of spring peepers, the statuesque form of the Great Blue Heron, and the haunting call of the Common Loon. It also means that non-wetland owners will be able to enjoy the attributes that have always made the Great Lakes State great: clear water, abundant fish and wildlife, and numerous recreational opportunities for visitors and residents alike.

State Agencies Involved in Wetland Protection and Management

Michigan Department of Environmental Quality
Land and Water Management Division
> P.O. Box 30458
> Lansing, MI 48909-7958
> PH: (517) 373-1170
> FX: (517) 373-9965

The Michigan Department of Environmental Quality (MDEQ), Land and Water Management Division (LWMD) administers several regulatory statutes that protect wetlands, including the following parts of P.A. 451 of 1994: Inland Lakes and Streams, the Great Lakes Submerged Lands, and Wetland Protection, among others. In addition, the MDEQ, LWMD

Land and Water Division
Michigan Department
of Environmental Quality

District Offices

NOTE: The location and phone numbers of these offices may change. If unable to obtain information at these locations, please contact the central office of Land and Water Management Division at (517) 373-1170.

also administers programs such as the P.A. 116 farmland easement program and Section 6217 of the Coastal Zone Act Reauthorization Amendments (see Chapter 10).

Offices

Marquette Office
1990 US-41 South
Marquette, MI 49855
PH: (906) 228-6561

Baraga and Crystal Falls Office
1420 US-2 West
Crystal Falls, MI 49920
PH: (906) 875-6622

Escanaba Office
6833 Highway 2, 41 & M-35
Gladstone, MI 49837
PH: (906) 786-2351

Ishpeming Office
1985 US-41 West
Ishpeming, MI 49849
PH: (906) 485-1031

Newberry Office
RR #4, P.O. Box 796
Newberry, MI 49868
PH: (906) 293-5131

Gaylord Office
P.O. Box 667
Gaylord, MI 49735
PH: (517) 732-3541

Cadillac Office
120 W. Chapin
Cadillac, MI 49601-2158
PH: (616) 775-9727

Mio Office
P.O. Box 939
191 S. Mt. Tom Road
Mio, MI 48647
PH: (517) 826-3211

Bay City Office
503 N. Euclid, Suite 1
Bay City, MI 48706
PH: (517) 684-9141

Grand Rapids Office
350 Ottawa, N.W.
Grand Rapids, MI 49503
PH: (616) 456-5071

Livonia Office
38980 Seven Mile Road
Livonia, MI 48152
PH: (313) 953-0241

Shiawassee Office
10650 S. Bennett Drive
Morrice, MI 48857
PH: (517) 625-4600

Plainwell Office
P.O. Box 355
Plainwell, MI 49080
PH: (616) 685-6851

Jackson Office
301 E. Louis Glick Hwy
Jackson, MI 49201
PH: (517) 780-7900
Lansing Office
P.O. Box 30458
Lansing, MI 48909-7958
PH: (517) 373-1170

Michigan Department of Environmental Quality Surface Water Quality Division

2nd Floor, Knapps Centre
Box 30273
Lansing, MI 48909-7773
PH: (517) 373-1949
FX: (517) 373-9958

The MDEQ, Surface Water Quality Division (SWQD) administers the National Pollution Discharge Elimination Permit program (which regulates pollutant discharges to surface water) and the grants program contained in Section 319 of the Clean Water Act. Staff can also provide information regarding impacts of activities to water quality.

Michigan Department of Natural Resources Wildlife Division

5th Floor, Mason Building
P.O. Box 30444
Lansing, MI 48909-7944
PH: (517) 335-1263
FX: (517) 373-6705

The Michigan Department of Natural Resources (MDNR) Wildlife Division is responsible for managing Michigan's wildlife resources. The Wildlife Division has restored or created thousands of acres of wetlands, administers Michigan's Endangered Species Protection Law and the Non-game Wildlife Fund Grants, and coordinates an amphibian monitoring program.

Offices

Upper Peninsula Field Headquarters
1990 US-41 South
Marquette, MI 49855
PH: (906) 228-6561

Baraga District Office
US-41 North, Box 440
Baraga, MI 49908
PH: (906) 353-6651

Crystal Falls District Office
1420 Highway US-2 West
Crystal Falls, MI 49920
PH: (906) 875-6622

Wildlife Division District Boundaries

Escanaba District Office
6833 Hwy 2, 41 & M-35
Gladstone, MI 49837
PH: (906) 786-2351

Newberry District Office
309 West McMillan Avenue
Newberry, MI 49868
PH: (906) 293-5131

Lower Peninsula Field Headquarters
P.O. Box 128
Roscommon, MI 48653
PH: (517) 275-5151

Gaylord District Office
1732 West M-32
P.O. Box 667
Gaylord, MI 49735
PH: (517) 732-3541

Cadillac District Office
8015 Mackinaw Trail
Cadillac, MI 49601
PH: (616) 775-9727

Mio District Office
191 S. Mt. Tom Road
Box 939
Mio, MI 48647
PH: (517) 826-3211

Bay City District Office
503 N. Euclid Avenue, Suite 1
Bay City, MI 48706
PH: (517) 684-9141

Grand Rapids District Office
State Office Building, 6th Floor
350 Ottawa, NW
Grand Rapids, MI 49503
PH: (616) 456-5071

Southeast Michigan District Office
38980 Seven Mile Road
Livonia, MI 48152
PH: (313) 953-0241

Shiawassee District Office
10650 S. Bennett Road
Morrice, MI 48857
PH: (517) 625-4600

Plainwell District Office
621 North 10th Street
P.O. Box 355
Plainwell, MI 49080
PH: (616) 685-6851

Jackson District Office
301 Louis Glick Hwy.
Jackson, MI 49201
PH: (517) 780-7900

**Michigan Department of Natural Resources
Forest Management Division**
8th Floor, Mason Building
Box 30452
Lansing, MI 48909-7952
PH: (517) 373-1275
FX: (517) 373-2443
The Michigan Department of Natural Resources
(MDNR) Forest Management Division administers
the federally funded Forest Stewardship Program
and the Stewardship Incentive Program.

Federal Agencies Involved in Wetland Protection and Management

U.S. Army Corps of Engineers
 Detroit District, Regulatory Branch
 P.O. Box 1027
 Detroit, MI 48231-1027
 PH: (313) 226-2218
 FX: (313) 226-6763
Under Section 404 of the Clean Water Act and pursuant regulations, the U.S. Army Corps of Engineers is authorized to issue permits for the discharge of dredged or fill material in waters of the United States, including wetlands. Upon request, the Corps will send public notices of projects to interested landowners.

Regulatory Branch Field Offices
Grand Haven Field Office
307 S. Harbor Street
Grand Haven, MI 49417
PH: (616) 842-5510

Saginaw Field Office
2445 Weadock Road
Essexville, MI 48732
PH: (517) 894-5451

Sault Ste. Marie Field Office
St. Mary's Falls Canal
Sault Ste. Marie, MI 49783
PH: (906) 635-3461

U.S. Environmental Protection Agency, Region 5, Watersheds and Nonpoint Source Programs Branch
 WW-16J, 77 West Jackson Boulevard
 Chicago, IL 60604
 PH: (312)-886-6115
 Wetlands Hotline: 1-800-832-7828
 FX: 312-886-7804
The U.S. Environmental Protection Agency (US EPA) is a regulatory agency with a role in state planning, wetland inventory activities, law enforcement, and preparation and distribution of educational materials. The US EPA has oversight of the Clean Water Act Section 404 wetlands program and establishes regional wetlands policies. The Agency works to protect the chemical, physical, and biological integrity of waters of the United States, including wetlands. Their Wetland Protection State Development Grant Program funds many valuable wetland protection and management activities in Michigan, including this guidebook.

U.S. Fish and Wildlife Service
 East Lansing Field Office
 2651 Coolidge Road
 East Lansing, MI 48823
 PH: (517) 351-2555
 FX: (517) 351-5419
The U.S. Fish and Wildlife Service's mission is to conserve, protect, and enhance fish and wildlife, and their habitats (including wetlands), for the continuing benefit of people. The Service works with federal, state, and local governments, as well as private interests, to restore, enhance, and protect wetlands. It provides technical assistance and consultation on wetland restorations, federal endangered and threatened species, and environmental contaminant issues to other governments and private landowners.

U.S.D.A. Michigan Farm Services Agency
 3001 Coolidge Road, Suite 100
 East Lansing, MI 48823-6321
 PH: (517) 337-6660
 FX: (517) 337-6898
The Farm Services Agency of the USDA administers the financial components of conservation provisions of the Farm Bill, including the Agricultural Conservation Program, the Conservation Reserve Program, and the Debt Cancellation Conservation Easements Program.

U.S.D.A. Natural Resources Conservation Service
 1405 S. Harrison Road, Room 101
 East Lansing, MI 48823-5243
 PH: (517) 337-6701
 FX: (517) 337-6905
The USDA Natural Resource Conservation Service (NRCS) is a technical agency which provides assistance to people to help conserve, improve, and sustain our resources and environment. The NRCS is responsible for identifying and delineating wetlands for purposes of the Wetland Provisions of the Farm Bills and Section 404 of the Clean Water Act on agricultural properties.

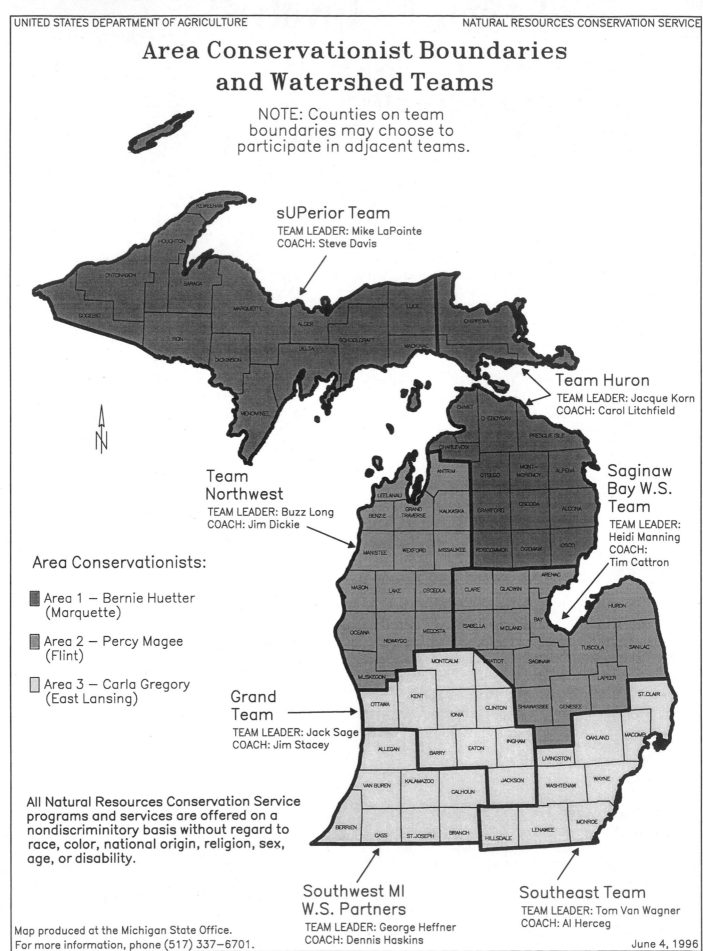

UNITED STATES DEPARTMENT OF AGRICULTURE

NATURAL RESOURCES CONSERVATION SERVICE

Area Conservationist Boundaries and Watershed Teams

NOTE: Counties on team boundaries may choose to participate in adjacent teams.

sUPerior Team
TEAM LEADER: Mike LaPointe
COACH: Steve Davis

Team Huron
TEAM LEADER: Jacque Korn
COACH: Carol Litchfield

Team Northwest
TEAM LEADER: Buzz Long
COACH: Jim Dickie

Saginaw Bay W.S. Team
TEAM LEADER: Heidi Manning
COACH: Tim Cattron

Area Conservationists:

■ Area 1 — Bernie Huetter (Marquette)

■ Area 2 — Percy Magee (Flint)

□ Area 3 — Carla Gregory (East Lansing)

Grand Team
TEAM LEADER: Jack Sage
COACH: Jim Stacey

All Natural Resources Conservation Service programs and services are offered on a nondiscriminitory basis without regard to race, color, national origin, religion, sex, age, or disability.

Southwest MI W.S. Partners
TEAM LEADER: George Heffner
COACH: Dennis Haskins

Southeast Team
TEAM LEADER: Tom Van Wagner
COACH: Al Herceg

Map produced at the Michigan State Office.
For more information, phone (517) 337-6701.

June 4, 1996

Non-Governmental Organizations that Provide Wetland Services

The organizations listed below are located across Michigan and provide a range of services for landowners. Typically, conservancies provide information regarding permanent protection options such as donation or conservation easements and offer field trips on their preserves. Organizations such as watershed councils may provide a range of services, including wetland delineation, design of wetland restoration projects, and information on wetland regulations. Other organizations listed here provide educational and volunteer opportunities for landowners and concerned citizens. Many organizations provide a combination of these services. If you want information regarding wetland protection on your property, or would like to get involved in community wetland protection efforts, please call the organization below that services your area.

Bear Creek Watershed Council
P.O. Box 357
Bear Lake, MI 49614
(616) 864-3228

The Bear Creek Watershed Council works to correct streambank erosion problems. The Council is also collecting information and mapping wetland areas within the Manistee County. They comment on state and federal dredge and fill applications.

Chippewa Watershed Conservancy
P.O. Box 896
Mt. Pleasant, MI 48804-0896
PH: (517) 644-5045
FX: (517) 774-6456

The mission of the Chippewa Watershed Conservancy is to protect the natural habitat within the watershed of the Chippewa River which encompasses Isabella, Midland, Mecosta, Clare, Montcalm, and Gratiot Counties. The Conservancy also works with the county park system to help them acquire land.

Citizens Against Pollution, Inc.
16311 Pine Street
Presque Isle, MI 49777-8652
(517) 595-6526

Citizens Against Pollution (CAP) was formed in 1990 to object to the siting of a pulp and paper mill in a predominantly wetland area of eastern Presque Isle County, along the Lake Huron shore. CAP is actively trying to get state acquisition of the area, with several inland lakes and miles of Lake Huron shoreline, as an addition to the state park.

Citizens for Alternatives to Chemical Contamination (CACC)
8735 Maple Grove Road
Lake, MI 48632-9511
PH: (517) 544-3318
FX: (517) 544-3318

CACC primarily serves as a clearinghouse between citizens and wetland protection resources. In addition, they have information on pending state and federal legislation.

Citizens for Environmental Protection
c/o M. Clark
27427 M-60 West
Cassopolis, MI 49031
PH: (616) 445-8769
FX: (616) 445-8987

Citizens for Environmental Protection works with other area groups to support specific legislative actions. The group sponsors conferences and workshops to bring information about wetlands to the general public.

Clean Water Action
4990 Northwind Drive, Suite 210
East Lansing, MI 48923
PH: (517) 337-4447
FX: (517) 337-2833

Clean Water Action (CWA) assists citizens' comments on dredge and fill applications and provides information on wetlands and water quality regulations (and pending legislation) at the state and federal level. CWA works to build coalitions and develop strategies for particular issues, provides assistance to citizens in preparing comments on legislation, and obtaining information from state and federal agencies, legislators, or other centralized sources.

Clinton River Watershed Council
　　1970 E. Auburn Road
　　Rochester Hills, MI 48307-4803
　　PH: (810) 853-9580
　　FX: (810) 853-0486
The Clinton River Watershed Council (CRWC) has provided assistance to local governments on wetland protection for decades. The Council conducts river corridor inventories in cooperation with local governments to identify appropriate local government action and has an "Adopt-A-Stream" program which includes associated wetlands. CRWC works with citizens and landowners to help solve environmental problems and developing strategies to meet environmental goals.

Concerned Citizens For West Bloomfield
　　5572 Stanhope Avenue
　　West Bloomfield, MI 48322
　　(810) 788-7145
Concerned Citizens for West Bloomfield was instrumental in getting a local wetland ordinance established. They have also been active in land acquisition in West Bloomfield Township. They regularly monitor the township wetland review board and also get involved with state and federal wetland issues.

DeGraaf Nature Center
　　600 Graffschap Road
　　Holland, MI 49423
　　(616) 355-1057
DeGraaf Nature Center is an Outdoor Classroom. The Center sponsors programs of an environmental nature and provides a meeting place for those interested in preserving the environment.

Detroit Audubon Society
　　1320 N. Campbell Road
　　Royal Oak, MI 48067-1555
　　PH: (810) 545-2929
　　FX: (810) 545-2860
Detroit Audubon Society (DAS) routinely comments on dredge and fill applications and assists citizens with their comments. DAS holds conservation easements, accepts donated properties statewide, and is assisting in developing a local land trust. DAS will also assist in site documentation, especially wildlife species.

Ducks Unlimited, Inc.
　　c/o Fred Hingst
　　12473 Tuscola
　　Clio, MI 48420
　　PH: (810) 686-5939
　　FX: (810) 686-9786
Ducks Unlimited, Inc. is a private, non-profit organization dedicated to conserving wetland habitat for waterfowl and other wildlife. Its mission is to fulfill the annual life cycle needs of North American waterfowl by protecting, enhancing, restoring, and managing important wetlands and associated uplands.

East Michigan Environmental Action Council (EMEAC)
　　21220 W. 14 Mile Road
　　Bloomfield Hills, MI 48301-4000
　　PH: (810) 258-5188
　　FX: (810) 258-5189
East Michigan Environmental Action Council assists citizens in work on local wetland issues. EMEAC also provides comment regarding pending local, state, and federal legislation.

Fernwood (Bontanic Garden & Nature Preserve)
　　13988 Range Line Road
　　Niles, MI 49120
　　PH: (616) 695-6491
　　FX: (616) 695-6688
Fernwood is a private, non-profit organization set on 105 acres of land that includes a 55-acre nature preserve. It promotes education, conservation, and appreciation of the natural world. Fernwood's location on the St. Joseph River and its proximity to Lake Michigan and Mud Lake Bog makes it an ideal setting for wetlands education.

Friends of Rose Township
　　9601 Fish Lake Road
　　Holly, MI 48442
　　(810) 634-7668
The Friends of Rose Township (FRT) comments on dredge and fill applications and assists citizens with their comments. The FRT also provides information about habitat preservation, grassroots wetlands protection initiatives, and educational materials.

Friends of the Crystal River
　　P.O. Box 123
　　Glen Arbor, MI 49636
　　(616) 334-4708
Friends of the Crystal River has focused the majority of their work on wetlands of the Crystal River

watershed. They have been involved in the contested case hearing process, circuit court litigation, and EPA oversight of MDEQ permitting actions.

Friends of the Rouge
950 Michigan Building
Detroit, MI 48226
PH: (313) 961-4050
FX: (313) 961-4018
Friends of the Rouge (FOR) focus their efforts on the Rouge River watershed. FOR works with local governments and provides basic information on wetland protection to landowners.

Galien River Watershed Council
P.O. Box 345
New Buffalo, MI 49117
The Galien River Watershed Council's (GRWC) educational programs focus on the identification and appreciation of wetlands and other natural resources in the area. GRWC also has a program to protect wetlands and floodplains through conservation easements, and will assist in developing local wetland protection ordinances.

Grand River Preservation Coalition
4642 Abrigador Trail, N.E.
Comstock Park, MI 49321
PH: (616) 784-6859
FX: (616) 784-4988
GRPC routinely comments on dredge and fill applications and assists citizens with their comments. GRPC also assists citizens and landowners with gathering information on local wetland issues throughout the Grand River watershed.

Grand Traverse Bay Watershed Initiative
1102 S. Cass Street, Suite B
Traverse City, MI 49684-3236
PH: (616) 935-1514
FX: (616) 922-4633
The Grand Traverse Bay Watershed Initiative is a long-term watershed management program based on local partnership agreements. The Initiative refers landowners to partner organizations that have wetland expertise.

Grand Traverse Regional Land Conservancy
624 Third Street
Traverse City, MI 49684
PH: (616) 929-7911
FX: (616) 929-0433
The mission of the Grand Traverse Regional Land Conservancy is to protect significant natural,

agricultural and scenic areas and advance land stewardship in Antrim, Benzie, Grand Traverse and Kalkaska counties - now and for future generations. They publish three issues yearly of the newletter *Landscript*. GTRLC accepts donations of land and conservation easements that meet their criteria.

Grass River Natural Area, Inc.
P.O. Box 231
Bellaire, MI 49615
(616) 533-8314
Grass River Natural Area, Inc. promotes the preservation, appreciation, and enjoyment of the environment in Antrim County and fosters an understanding of the interrelationships of natural resources through education, scientific research, and passive recreation. The Natural Area gives numerous field trips and events as part of spring and summer educational programs and also provides field trips upon request.

The Great Lakes Bioregional Land Conservancy
4107 Columbiaville Rd.
Columbiaville, MI 48421
(810) 793-2511
The mission of The Great Lakes Bioregional Land Conservancy is to: 1) Protect farmland and open space that contribute to a healthy and sustainable natural environment, and 2) support land stewardship centers as places where people can learn to live more in harmony with nature in Southeastern Michigan. Great Lakes Bioregional Land Conservancy accepts donations of land and conservation easements that meet their criteria.

Grosse Ile Nature and Land Conservancy
P.O. Box 12
Grosse Ile, MI 48138
PH: (313) 676-6657
FX: (313) 671-1138
The mission of the Grosse Ile Nature and Land Conservancy is to carry on a program of acquisition, maintenance, and protection of Grosse Ile's natural resources and to engage in a program of education regarding those resources. The Conservancy publishes quarterly The Newsletter of the Grosse Ile Nature and Land Conservancy. GIN&LC accepts donations of land and conservation easements that meet their criteria.

Headwaters Environmental Station

HCR 1 Box 98A, Keweenaw Bioregion
Toivola, MI 49965
(906) 288-3000

Headwaters Environmental Station is a non-profit educational facility. The 160-acre Field Station is located at the headwaters of the Elm and Little Elm Rivers. Headwaters' programs focus on the importance of watersheds and a bioregional view.

Headwaters Land Conservancy

P.O. Box 457
Gaylord, MI 49735
PH: (517) 732-3551 or 826-5714
FX: (517) 732-5578

The mission of the Headwaters Land Conservancy is to use a participatory approach to securing and sustaining the quality of life enjoyed by present and future residents of northeast lower Michigan covering Alcona, Alpena, Arenac, Crawford, Iosco, Montmorency, Ogemaw, Oscoda, Otsego, Presque Isle, and Roscommon Counties. The Conservancy seeks to foster an open-space philosophy and preserve ecologically sensitive areas, scenic landscapes, and historic features - together with associated natural resources, archaeological legacy, and recreational opportunity. HLC accepts donations of land and conservation easements that meet their criteria.

Huron River Watershed Council

1100 North Main Street, Suite 210
Ann Arbor, MI 48104-1059
PH: (313) 769-5123
FX: (313) 998-0163

The Huron River Watershed Council (HRWC) routinely comments on dredge and fill applications and assists citizens with their comments. HRWC's "Adopt-A-Waterway" program encourages and trains citizens to assess watershed land use patterns, develop wetland protection workplans, implement those workplans, and monitor wetland plant and animal populations. HRWC also has a program to protect wetlands and floodplains through conservation easements, and will assist in developing local wetland protection ordinances.

Independence Land Conservancy

P.O. Box 285
Clarkston, MI 48347
PH: (810) 625-8193
FX: (810) 625-9170

The mission of the Independence Land Conservancy is to preserve for the general public the natural and historic resources of Independence Township, and adjacent communities. They publish annually Scenic Vistas. The Conservancy gives biannual field trips on its three 30-acre preserves. ILC accepts donations of land and conservation easements that meet their criteria.

Indian Springs Metropark Nature Center

5200 Indian Trail
White Lake, MI 48386
PH: (810) 625-7280
FX: (810) 625-6639

The Indian Springs Nature Center provides wetland programs and exhibits that are generally centered around the Huron Swamp, which is located in the park. These wetlands are the headwaters of the Huron River and home to many wetland plants and animals. The Nature Center's programs often discuss the importance of such areas for biodiversity and water quality.

Inland Seas Education Association

P.O. Box 218
Suttons Bay, MI 49682
PH: (616) 271-3077
FX: (616) 271-3088

Inland Seas Education Association (ISEA) works to build stewardship for the Great Lakes through citizen education. Coastal wetlands education is an important part of ISEA's work.

Kalamazoo Nature Center

7000 N. Westnedge Avenue
Kalamazoo, MI 49004
PH: (616) 381-1574
FX: (616) 381-2557

The Kalamazoo Nature Center is an educational facility that sponsors programs and activities on a wide range of environmental topics. Staff assist citizens with wetland-related questions, conduct workshops and seminars, and school-age programs. Many wetland related informational resources are available for use by citizens and landowners.

Lake Erie Advisory Committee

47 East Elm
Monroe, MI 48161
PH: (313) 242-0909
FX: (313) 457-2005

The Lake Erie Advisory Committee acts as a liaison between local conservation groups on matters relating to preservation and protection of the Erie marshes. The Lake Erie Advisory Committee is associated with the Lake Erie Clean-Up Committee,

Inc., that encourages citizen involvement in the protection of natural resources.

Lake Michigan Federation
   161 Muskegon Mall, Suite 502
   Muskegon, MI 49440
   PH: (616) 722-5116
   FX: (616) 722-4918
The Lake Michigan Federation (LMF) routinely comments on dredge and fill applications and assists citizens with their comments. LMF is currently coordinating a wetland and habitat assessment of the White Lake Watershed.

Lake St. Clair Advisory Committee
   P.O. Box 272
   Mt. Clemens, MI 48046
   (810) 725-8827
The Lake St. Clair Advisory Committee is a conservation group dedicated to the preservation of the waters, wetlands, and wildlife of Lake St. Clair. The Committee participates in preparing the St. Clair River and Clinton River Remedial Action Plans.

League of Women Voters of Michigan
   200 Museum Drive, Suite 202
   Lansing, MI 48933
   PH: (517) 484-5383
   FX: (517) 484-3086
The League of Women Voters mainly deals with legislation affecting wetlands, rather than individual wetland cases. Their Citizen Information Center provides legislative updates and reference referrals.

Leelanau Conservancy
   P.O. Box 1007
   Leland, MI 49654
   PH: (616) 256-9665
   FX: (616) 256-9693
The mission of the Leelanau Conservancy is to preserve land, water, and historic resources of Leelanau County. The Conservancy publishes three issues per year of the Leelanau Conservancy. They conduct 20 field trips on their preserves annually. LC accepts donations of land and conservation easements that meet their criteria and offers free ecological evaluations of qualified wetland parcels.

Les Cheneaux Foundation
   c/o 500 North Western Avenue, Suite 204
   Lake Forest, IL 60045
   Cedarville, MI 49719
   PH: (708) 735-8764
   FX: (708) 735-8770

This mission of the Les Cheneaux Foundation is to preserve natural areas and open space in and near Les Cheneaux Islands. LCF accepts donations of land that meet their criteria.

Liaison for Inter-Neighborhood Cooperation (LINC)
   P.O. Box 40
   Okemos, MI 48805
   (517) 349-4306
LINC is a civic improvement organization that supports the protection of natural resources and sound land use planning. They promote these concerns through community involvement, networking, and civic participation.

Little Traverse Conservancy
   3264 Powell Road
   Harbor Springs, MI 49740
   PH: (616) 347-0991
   FX: (616) 347-5928
The mission of the Little Traverse Conservancy is to protect the natural diversity and beauty of northern Michigan encompassing Charlevoix, Emmet, Cheboygan, Chippewa, and Mackinac counties by preserving significant land and scenic areas, and fostering appreciation and understanding of the environment. They publish quarterly the Update. The Conservancy gives numerous field trips and accepts donations of land and conservation easements that meet their criteria. They also assist other groups to pre-acquire, handle negotiations, secure donations/bargain sales, and also assist with grant applications.

Livingston Land Conservancy
   P.O. Box 1424
   Brighton, MI 48116
   PH: (810) 229-4141
   FX: (810) 229-4143
The mission of the Livingston Land Conservancy (a committee of the Southeast Michigan Land Conservancy) is to preserve the rural character and natural heritage of Livingston County.

Metro Beach Nature Center
   31300 Metro Parkway
   P.O. Box 1037
   Mt. Clemens, MI 48046
   PH: (810) 463-4332
   FX: (810) 463-6630
The Metro Beach Nature Center consists of wetlands that are a part of the last coastal wetland area in Macomb County. The Center gives group ap-

pointments with wetland themes to school and scout groups, and it also conducts family programs.

Michigan Association of Conservation Districts

P.O. Box 539
Lake City, MI 49651
PH: (616) 839-3360
FX: (616) 839-3361

The Michigan Association of Conservation Districts is a nongovernmental, nonprofit, 501(c)(3) organization established in 1940 to represent and provide services to Michigan's 82 Soil and Water Conservation Districts. Many of the local districts have some form of wetland program, including review of dredge and fill permits, wetland restoration, educational workshops, and assistance in applying for permits.

Michigan Audubon Society

6011 W. St. Joseph
P.O. Box 80527
Lansing, MI 48908-0527
PH: (517) 886-9144
FX: (517) 886-9466

The mission of the Michigan Audubon Society is to promote the awareness, understanding, enjoyment, and stewardship of the environment and natural resources of the upper Great Lakes Region by educating the public, supporting ecological research, maintaining sanctuaries, and by taking part in appropriate advocacy to protect the environment, with an emphasis on birds and their habitats. The Society publishes biannually The Jack-Pine Warbler and Michigan Birds and Natural History. MAS accepts donations of land and conservation easements that meet their criteria.

Michigan Duck Hunters Association-Wayne

31012 Windsor
Westland, MI 48185
(313) 421-6452

The Michigan Duck Hunters Association of Wayne County works for the protection and restoration of wetlands, with an emphasis on waterfowl habitat.

Michigan Environmental Council

115 West Allegan, Suite 10B
Lansing, MI 48933
PH: (517) 487-9539
FX: (517) 487-9541

The Michigan Environmental Council (MEC) distributes information to its member groups about proposed or pending legislation, including that concerning wetlands. MEC also suggests coordinated action in response to such proposals. Lansing MEC staff advocate for improved state and federal wetland regulations on behalf of their member groups.

Michigan Lakes & Streams Associations, Inc.

P.O. Box 249
Three Rivers, MI 49093
PH: (616) 273-8200
FX: (616) 273-2919

The Michigan Lake and Stream Associations, Inc. (ML&SA) serves as a communication link between hundreds of individual lake associations throughout Michigan. ML&SA advises citizens on understanding wetland regulations and on the best approaches to avoid or minimize wetland destruction.

Michigan Nature Association

7981 Beard Road, P.O. Box 102
Avoca, MI 48006
PH: (810) 324-2626
FX: (810) 324-2345

This mission of Michigan Nature Association is to a) carry on a program of natural history study and conservation education, and b) to acquire, maintain, and protect nature sanctuaries, natural areas, and plant preserves in the State of Michigan or areas adjacent thereto. They publish the MNA Members Newsletter five times a year. MNA accepts donations of land and conservation easements that meet their criteria.

Michigan Natural Areas Council

c/o Matthaei Botanical Gardens
1800 N. Dixboro Road
Ann Arbor, MI 48105-9741
(313) 461-9390

The Michigan Natural Areas Council is made up of individual members statewide, including naturalists, scientists, academics, etc. The Council's focus is to promote the protection of significant natural areas in Michigan and to provide information to the public.

Michigan United Conservation Clubs

2101 Wood Street
P.O. Box 30235
Lansing, MI 48909
PH: (517) 371-1041
FX: (517) 371-1505

The Michigan United Conservation Clubs (MUCC) routinely comments on dredge and fill applications and assists citizens with their comments. MUCC's Wetland Watch program provides local activists across the state with public notices and technical assistance free of charge. MUCC Lansing staff work to protect wetlands at the local, state, and federal levels. In addition, MUCC has over 450 affiliate organizations across the state, many of which also work on wetlands.

Michigan Waterfowl Association

c/o Steve Healy, President
P.O. Box 163
Marquette, MI 49855
PH: (616) 228-7545
FX: (906) 228-4834 Attn: Bob Dupras

Members of the Michigan Waterfowl Association attend and speak at public meetings concerning protection of wetland resources.

Michigan Wildlife Habitat Foundation

6425 S. Pennsylvania, Suite 9
Lansing, MI 48911
PH: (517) 882-3110
FX: (517) 882-3687

The Michigan Wildlife Habitat Foundation provides citizens with design, technical, and funding assistance, supervision of fish and wildlife restorations, and community improvements. The Foundation sponsors an annual training seminar to teach people to recognize drained wetlands that can be restored or improved.

Mid-Michigan Environmental Action Council (Mid-MEAC)

P.O. Box 27555
Lansing, MI 48909-7555
PH: (517) 337-2237
FX: (517) 337-2833

Mid-MEAC will provide guidance and information to landowners on water quality, wetland protection, and other environmental issues. The organization also promotes public awareness through events, workshops, presentations, and their monthly newsletter, *Mid-MEAC Environmental News*.

National Wildlife Federation

Great Lakes Natural Resource Center
506 East Liberty
Ann Arbor, MI 48104-2210
PH: (313) 769-3351
FX: (313) 769-1449

The National Wildlife Federation (NWF), founded in 1936, has 4 million supporters across the country. NWF's Great Lakes Natural Resource Center has information on the Section 404 program and other wetland educational materials available for land-

owners and citizens. NWF plays a critical role at the state, regional, and federal level to ensure that wetland protection regulations are fair and effective.

Natural Areas Association

P.O. Box 154
Okemos, MI 48805-0154
(517) 332-7960

The Natural Areas Association is a charitable trust which supports conservation of the natural environmental heritage through increased public awareness, education, and acquisition of public and private natural areas.

Natural Areas Conservancy of West Michigan, Inc. (NACOWMI)

1432 Wealthy S.E., Suite L-3
Grand Rapids, MI 49506
PH: (616) 451-9476
FX: (616) 451-3054

The mission of NACOWMI is to preserve lands that arc important for their values as habitat for native plants and animals, as centers for study, quiet recreation, and scenic beauty in Ottawa, Kent, Muskegon, Newaygo, and Oceana Counties, plus the northern half of Allegan County. They publish quarterly the *NACOWMI Landmarks*. The Association gives four or more field trips annually. NACOWMI accepts donations of land and conservation easements that meet their criteria.

Northern Michigan Environmental Action Council (NMEAC)

P.O. Box 1166
Traverse City, MI 49685-1166
(616) 946-6931

NMEAC will assist citizens with commenting on dredge and fill applications and developing wetland protection strategies.

North Woods Conservancy

P.O. Box 124
Calumet, MI 49913
(906) 337-0782

The mission of the North Woods Conservancy is to protect and enhance native biological diversity and encourage low-impact living in western Upper Peninsula (primarily Houghton, Keweenaw, Baraga, and Marquette Counties). NWC accepts donations of land and conservation easements that meet their criteria.

Oakland Land Conservancy

798 W. Gunn Road
Rochester, MI 48306
PH: (810) 652-4903
FX: (810) 652-4903

The mission of the Oakland Land Conservancy is to work toward the protection and preservation of natural areas throughout Oakland County. OLC accepts donations of land and conservation easements that meet their criteria.

Old Mission Conservancy

P.O. Box 88
Old Mission, MI 49673
PH: (616) 947-0597
FX: (616) 947-1684

The mission of the Old Mission Conservancy is to work toward preservation of agricultural lands, scenic vistas, shoreline, and wetlands in Peninsula Township (Old Mission Peninsula). They function in conjunction with the Grand Traverse Regional Land Conservancy. OMC accepts donations of land and conservation easements that meet their criteria.

Pere Marquette Watershed Council, Inc.

P.O. Box 212
Baldwin, MI 49304
(616) 745-7692

The Pere Marquette Watershed Council strives to protect the natural state of the Pere Marquette River system, to preserve and foster its great natural beauty, and to keep it free from all artificial and unnatural practices which may threaten its natural and free-flowing state. The Council gathers and disseminates information and works to educate the public concerning the Pere Marquette River system.

Pheasants Forever, Inc.

c/o Jim Goodheart
Michigan Field Representative
8401 Stoney Creek Ct.
Davison, MI 48423
(810) 658-2209

Pheasants Forever, Inc. is a non-profit organization dedicated to preserving, creating, and enhancing wildlife habitat. The Michigan chapters raise money and keep those funds locally to improve the land's carrying capacity for primarily the ring-necked pheasant, but also for other species that associate in these habitats. Pheasants Forever, Inc. assists landowners working to restore or enhance wetlands with advice, funding, seed sources, etc.

Points Betsie to Sable Conservancy, Inc.

P.O. Box 705
Manistee, MI 49660
PH: (616) 723-9911
FX: (616) 723-9914

The mission of the Points. Betsie to Sable Conservancy is to protect the natural features of Manistee, Mason, and Benzie Counties. PBSC accepts donations of land and conservation easements that meet their criteria.

Potawatomi Land Trust

P.O. Box 130122
Ann Arbor, MI 48113-0122
(313) 449-7229

The mission of Potawatomi Land Trust (PLT) is to Protect farmland, natural areas, and open space in Washtenaw County. They publish *The PLT Newsletter* three times a year. PLT accepts donations of land and conservation easements that meet their criteria.

Rails-to-Trails Conservancy, Michigan Chapter

913 W. Holmes, Suite 145
Lansing, MI 48910
PH: (517) 393-6022
FX: (517) 393-1960

The mission of the Rails-to-Trails Conservancy, Michigan Chapter is to enhance America's communities and countrysides by converting thousands of miles of abandoned rail corridors, and connecting open space into a nationwide network of public trails. They publish Trailblazer, quarterly and Trailblazing in Michigan, periodically.

Raisin Valley Land Trust

P.O. Box 419
Manchester, MI 48158
(517) 456-4901, (313) 428-8108

The mission of the Raisin Valley Land Trust (RVLT) is to preserve natural, agricultural, and historical character of the upper River Raisin watershed which encompasses the Upper River Raisin watershed, S.W. Washtenaw, N.W. Lenawee, and S.E. Jackson counties. They publish quarterly the RVLT Newsletter. RVLT accepts donations of land and conservation easements that meet their criteria.

Saginaw Bay Advisory Council

P.O. Box 643
Bay City, MI 48707
(517) 893-3782

The Saginaw Bay Advisory Council is made up of people from all around the Saginaw Bay area. The

Council will provide consultation to landowners seeking wetland permits. Public Notices for dredge and fill applications are thoroughly reviewed and often commented upon by members.

Saginaw Bay Visitor Center
3582 State Park Drive
Bay City, MI 48706
PH: (517) 667-0717
FX: (517) 667-0742

Saginaw Bay Visitor Center, with adjacent Tobico Marsh, plays an important role in educating the younger generation. By ensuring that students understand the significance of wetlands and the roles they play within the ecosystem, the Center gives the youngsters a foundation for becoming respectful and conscientious adults.

Partnership for Saginaw Bay Watershed
Pioneer Annex 9A
Saginaw Valley State University
University Center, MI 48710
(517) 791-7367

The Partnership for Saginaw Bay Watershed provides educational materials on wetlands and water resources to interested citizens and local officials. The Council sponsors an "Adopt-A-Stream" program, school river monitoring, and workshops on local zoning ordinances to protect water resources.

Sarett Nature Center
2300 Benton Center Road
Benton Harbor, MI 49022
PH: (616) 927-4832
FX: (616) 927-2742

Sarett Nature Center is a living wetland lab with swamp forest, shrub carr, sedge meadow, marsh, ponds, and fen all along the Paw Paw River. The Center has five miles of trails and many boardwalks through the wetlands.

Save Our Shorelines, Inc.
2447 Lakeshore Drive
Muskegon, MI 49441
(616) 755-3215

Save Our Shorelines (SOS), Inc. monitors all requests to the Michigan DNR or Army Corps of Engineers to fill, excavate, or change wetland conditions.

Scio Open Space Conservation Committee
4500 W. Liberty Rd.
Ann Arbor, MI 48103

The mission of the Scio Open Space Conservation Committee (SOSCC) is to work to preserve valuable open spaces and natural features in Scio Township, now largely in conjunction with the Potawatomi Land Trust. SOSCC accepts donations of land and conservation easements that meet their criteria.

Seven Ponds Nature Center
3854 Crawford Road
Dryden, MI 48428
(810) 796-3200

Seven Ponds Nature Center is a 273-acre nature sanctuary and environmental education center. The property contains excellent examples of glacial lakes, marshes, streams, and ponds. The Center offers ecologically oriented programs to school groups and the general public. Many of these programs relate directly to wetlands.

Sierra Club, Mackinac Chapter
300 N. Washington Sq. #411
Lansing, MI 48933
PH: (517) 484-2372
FX: (517) 484-3108

The Sierra Club, Mackinaw Chapter and its regional groups across Michigan can assist groups and individuals with communicating their concerns about wetlands policy to elected officials at all levels. The Sierra Club pursues litigation where necessary. The Mackinac Chapter does provide legislative alerts issued by the Great Lakes Program or the national office.

Society of Wetland Scientists (SWS)
North Central Chapter
P.O. Box 1122
Big Rapids, MI 49307
PH: (616) 796-4540
FX: (616) 796-4564

SWS has six objectives: 1) to provide an independent forum for interchange of ideas and data in wetland science, 2) to develop and encourage wetland science as a distinct discipline, 3) to encourage and evaluate the educational, scientific, and technological development of all branches of wetland science and practice, 4) to encourage the knowledgeable husbandry of wetland resources, 5) to encourage a fraternity of scientists based on shared knowledge, dedication, friendship, and mutual respect, and 6) to evolve an organizational credo or code of practice based on a shared ethic.

Southeast Michigan Land Conservancy

6410 St. Mary's
Detroit, MI 48228
(313) 582-8377

The mission of the Southeast Michigan Land Conservation (SMLC) is to protect parks, open space, and natural areas in the seven-county southeast Michigan region being Wayne, Oakland, Macomb, Washtenaw, Monroe, Livingston, and St. Clair Counties. They publish one to three times a year the *SMLC Newsletter*. SMLC gives 4 field trips annually. SMLC protects wetlands by direct purchase and accepts donations of land and conservation easements that meet their criteria.

Southwest Michigan Land Conservancy

8135 Cox's Drive
Suite 106
Portage, MI 49002-5879
PH: (616) 324-1600
FX: (616) 324-9760

The mission of the Southwest Michigan Land Conservancy (SWMLC) is to protect the natural beauty and diversity of southwest Michigan covering Allegan, Barry, Berrien, Branch, Calhoun, Cass, Kalamazoo, St. Joseph, and Van Buren Counties by preserving significant land and scenic areas, and fostering appreciation for and understanding of the environment. They publish the Deeds quarterly. SWMLC accepts donations of land and conservation easements that meet their criteria.

Superior Land Conservancy (SLC)

8615 Cherry Hill Rd.
Ypsilanti, MI 48198
PH: (313) 482-5957
FX: (313) 845-9778

SLC is a committee of the Southeast Michigan Land Conservancy. The mission of SLC is to help articulate, organize, and implement strategies for preserving agricultural and natural areas between the converging cities of Detroit, Ypsilanti and Ann Arbor. They publish the *SLC Update* twice yearly. In the spring, summer, and fall SLC offers fields trips. SLC accepts donations of land and conservation easements that meet their criteria.

The Nature Conservancy, Michigan Chapter

2840 East Grand River Ave., Suite 5
East Lansing, MI 48823
PH: (517) 332-1741
FX: (517) 332-8382

The mission of The Nature Conservancy (TNC), Michigan Chapter is to preserve plants, animals, and natural communities that represent the diversity of life on Earth by protecting the lands and waters they need to survive throughout Michigan. They publish quarterly the Michigan Conservancy. The Conservancy gives 15 field trips annually. TNC accepts donations of land and purchase lands that meet their criteria. The provide assistance to other groups, including development of management plans, land management, and ecological expertise.

Thunder Bay River Watershed Council

P.O. Box 751
Alpena, MI 49707

The Thunder Bay River Watershed Council is a volunteer organization working to protect water resources in the Thunder Bay River watershed.

Tip of the Mitt Watershed Council

P.O. Box 300
Conway, MI 49722
PH: (616) 347-1181
FX: (616) 347-5928

Tip of the Mitt Watershed Council (TOMWC) offers an "Adopt-A-Stream" program that includes associated wetlands, a "Wetland Stewardship" program, a planning and zoning program to promote wetland and water quality protection, and a wetland delineation service on private properties. Staff design wetland restoration, enhancement, and creation projects. TOMWC also publishes *Great Lakes Wetlands*, the *Citizens' Wetlands Report and Habitat News*, and coordinates the Great Lakes Aquatic Habitat Network and Fund.

Trout Unlimited

6815 Clubhouse Drive W
Stanwood, MI 49346
(616) 972-2737

Trout Unlimited (TU) works to enhance, protect, and restore our cold water resources. This advocacy includes work for the protection of wetlands in conjunction with cold and cool water resources. TU works with landowners, various government agencies, other environmental groups, and the court system to provide this protection.

Upper Peninsula Env. Coalition (UPEC)

P.O. Box 847
Marquette, MI 49855
PH: (906) 524-5441
FX: (906) 524-5441

UPEC receives dredge and fill applications for the entire upper peninsula of Michigan and either provides comments or refers them to appropriate agencies and individuals. UPEC also helps to coordinate and develop action strategies for particular wetland protection issues.

Washtenaw Land Conservancy, Inc.

c/o First Martin Corporation
115 Depot Street
Ann Arbor, MI 48104
PH: (313) 994-5050
FX: (313) 761-6151

The mission of the Washtenaw Land Conservancy, Inc. is to preserve land for public use. They publish and annual membership letter and accept donations of land and conservation easements that meet their criteria.

Water and Air Team for Charlevoix (WATCH)

P.O. Box 615
Charlevoix, MI 49720
(616) 547-5530

WATCH routinely comments on dredge and fill applications and assists citizens with their comments as much as possible. WATCH's "Adopt-A-Stream" program can be expanded to include wetlands, and they are available to help in litigation or contested case hearings.

West Bloomfield Land Conservancy

7379 Edinborough Drive
West Bloomfield, MI 48322
PH: (810) 661-6162
FX: (810) 661-6184

The West Bloomfield Land Conservancy has assisted in protecting two major park sites that have extensive wetland areas. The Conservancy does not currently hold any easements or deeds to land, although it could if certain criteria were met. Work to date has consisted primarily of education and advocacy.

West Michigan Environmental Action Council (WMEAC)

1432 Wealthy Street, S.E.
Grand Rapids, MI 49506
PH: (616) 451-3051
FX: (616) 451-3054

WMEAC routinely comments on dredge and fill applications and assists citizens with their comments whenever possible. WMEAC's "Adopt-A-Stream" program includes wetlands. WMEAC's wetland protection activities include publishing issue alerts and fact sheets, providing speakers, working with media, coalition building, strategic planning, and policy development.

Wetlands Conservation Association

P.O. Box 133
Stevensville, MI 49127-0133
(616) 429-1862

The Wetlands Conservation Association (WCA) routinely comments on dredge and fill applications and assists citizens with their comments. The Association is developing a conservation easement program and is actively pursuing wetland restoration projects. WCA is also active in providing wetland protection advice to citizens.

Wildlife Unlimited-Delta County

6604 N Road
Escanaba, MI 49829
(906) 786-1354

Wildlife Unlimited of Delta County is a 500 member non-profit organization dedicated to the preservation and restoration of wildlife habitat in the area of Delta County, Michigan. Attention is currently being directed toward the Ford River Delta, one of three extensive wetlands in the area.

With the Grain

P.O. Box 517
Mattawan, MI 49071-0517
(616) 624-1140

With the Grain is a non-profit organization dedicated to educating people about their effect on the environment and motivating them to make informed, responsible decisions. With the Grain evaluates the thinking behind individual, business, and municipal decisions, advocates long-term planning for natural resource preservation, and encourages individual self-empowerment.

Yellow Dog Watershed Preserve, Inc.

County Road 550, Box 99
Marquette, MI 49855
(906) 228-8485

The mission of the Yellow Dog Watershed Preserve, Inc. is to acquire, hold, and preserve parcels of real property in the watershed and its tributaries through land trust deeds and conservation easements for the benefit of the general public. YDWP publishes a newsletters six times yearly and accepts donations of land and conservation easements that meet their criteria.

Glossary

Acid - A substance which yields positively charged Hydrogen ions when in solution.

Acidic - Solutions (including soil moisture and water vapor) which have a pH value less than 7.

Acidophilic Vegetation (Acidophile) - Vegetation adapted to living in acidic conditions.

Aerobic - A condition in which molecular oxygen is a part of the environment and freely available to organisms.

Alkali (Base) - A substance which yields negatively charged hydroxide or carbonate ions when in solution.

Alkaline (Basic) - Solutions (including soil moisture and water vapor) which have a pH value greater than 7.

Anaerobic - A condition in which molecular oxygen is absent (or effectively so) from the environment.

Aquifer - A geologic formation that is capable of yielding a significant amount of ground water to a well or spring.

Bog - A peatland which is isolated from ground or surface water (only significant water inputs are directly from rain) and dominated by mosses (Sphagnum spp.), sedges, shrubs, sedges, and evergreen trees such as black spruce and tamarack.

Buttressed - The swollen or enlarged bases of trees developed in response to wet conditions or prolonged inundation.

Calcareous - Containing calcium carbonate, calcium, or lime which typically causes an alkaline condition.

Concentric - A series of circles, each progressively smaller, nested inside one another.

Detritus - Any non-living plant or animal material.

Drained, effectively - A condition where ground or surface water has been removed by artificial means to the point that an area no longer meets the wetland hydrology criterion.

Drift line - A accumulation of water-carried debris along a topographical contour of the land surface or on vegetation that provides direct evidence of prior inundation and often indicates the directional flow of flood waters.

Ecological Integrity - A term used to describe intact ecosystems that are diverse, productive, and otherwise function normally.

Ecosystem - A community of plants and animals and the physical environment they inhabit, e.g., wetlands, rivers, upland. The ecosystem reflects the interaction among soil, climate, vegetation , and animal life.

Erosion - The process by which soil particles are detached and transported by water, ice, wind, and gravity down slope or to some downstream point.

Eutrophication - Process by which a body of water becomes highly productive either due to natural causes or excessive inputs of pollution rich in dissolved nutrients.

Evapotranspiration- Conversion of liquid water to vapor both by evaporation and by transpiration of the water by plants growing thereon.

Facultative Plant Species (FAC) - Plant species that are estimated to occur in wetlands approximately 34-66% of the time.

Facultative Upland Plant Species (FACU) -Plant species that are estimated to occur in wetlands approximately 1-33% of the time.

Facultative Wetland Plant Species (FACW) - Plant species that are estimated to occur in wetlands approximately 67-99% of the time.

Fen - A type of peatland that receives mineral-rich inputs of ground or surface water and dominated by sedges and other grass-like vegetation.

Field Tiles (Drainage Tiles) - Perforated plastic or clay pipes that are buried under the surface of the ground to facilitate drainage.

Flora - Plant life.

Gleyed - Distinctive blueish-gray soil color which develops under conditions of poor drainage, resulting in reduction of iron and other elements.

Ground water - Water that seeps below the surface of the ground and fills interconnected pores in soil and cracks in rocks.

Growing season - The portion of the year when soil temperatures are above biologic zero (41 degrees F) as defined by "Soil Taxonomy."

Habitat - The environment in which the requirements of a specific plant or animal are met.

Herb - Nonwoody plants including grasses and grass-like plants, forbs, ferns, fern allies, and nonwoody vines. For the purposes wetland delineation, seedlings of woody plants that are less than three feet in height are also considered herbs.

Hydric soil - A soil that is saturated, flooded, or ponded long enough during the growing season to develop anaerobic conditions in the root zone.

Hydrology - The science dealing with the properties, distribution, and circulation of water.

Hydroperiod - The duration of a particular flooding event. The period during which surface water remains on a wetland.

Hydrophyte or Hydrophytic Vegetation: Literally, water-loving vegetation. Any macrophyte that grows in water, or on a substrate that is at least periodically deficient in oxygen as a result of excessive water content; plants typically found in wetlands and other aquatic habitats.

Indicator - An event, entity, or condition that typically characterizes a prescribed environment or situation; indicators determine or aid in determining whether or not certain circumstances exist or criteria are satisfied.

Infiltration - The downward movement of water from the atmosphere into soil and rock formations.

Interdunal Swale - A type of wetland usually dominated by grass-like vegetation that occurs between sand dunes and beach ridges along the Great Lakes shoreline.

Macrophyte - Any plant species that can be readily observed without the aid of optical magnification, including all vascular plant species or bryophytes (e.g. Sphagnum spp.), as well as large algae (e.g. Chara spp., and Fucus spp.).

Mineral soil - Any soil consisting primarily of mineral (sand, silt, and clay) material, rather than organic matter.

Mottles - Spots or blotches of different color or shades of color interspersed within the dominant matrix color in a soil layer.

Muck - Dark colored, finely textured, well-decomposed organic soil material.

Nonhydric soil - A soil that has developed under predominantly aerobic conditions.

Nonwetland - Any area that has sufficiently dry conditions that hydrophytic vegetation, hydric soils, and/or wetland hydrology are lacking, including former wetlands that have been effectively drained (synonymous with Upland).

Nutrient - Any mineral, compound, or element that promotes biological growth or development.

Obligate Upland Plant Species (UPL) - Plant species that are estimated to occur in wetlands less than 1% of the time.

Obligate Upland Plant Species (UPL) - Plant species that are estimated to occur in wetlands less than 1% of the time.

Obligate Wetland Species (OBL) - Plant species that are estimated to occur in wetlands more than 99% of the time.

Oxidation-Reduction - A complex of biochemical reactions that influence the valence state of elements and their ions. Long periods of soil saturation during the growing season tend to elicit anaerobic conditions that shift the overall process to a reducing condition.

Oxidized Root Channels - Iron oxide concretions (orange or red-brown in color) that form along the length of a root channel in wetland conditions. Oxidized rhizospheres serve as a common field indicator of wetland hydrology in mineral soils.

Peat - A low-density, slightly decomposed fibrous organic soil composed largely of plant material.

Peatland - A generic term used to refer to peat accumulating wetlands, such as fens and bogs.

Perennial (plant) - Living for more than one year.

Permeability - The quality of the soil that enables water to move downward through the profile, measured as the number of inches per hour that water moves downward through the saturated soil.

Piezometer - A shallow well used to measure ground water fluctuations.

Plant Community - The various plant species that share a single habitat.

Propagules - The structure of an organism involved in dispersal and reproduction, as in seeds or spores of plants.

Rhizoshpere - The zone of a soil in which interactions between living plant roots and micro-organisms occur; root zone.

Riparian - Adjacent to a body of water; a person who resides on a shoreline property.

Sapling - Woody vegetation between 0.4 and 5.0 inches in diameter at breast height and greater than or equal to 20 feet in height, not including woody vines.

Saturated - A condition in which virtually all voids (pores) between soil particles are temporarily or permanently filled with water.

Shrub - Woody vegetation usually greater than 3 feet but less than 20 feet tall, including multi-stemmed, bushy shrubs and small trees and saplings.

Staff Gauge - A fixed point in a body of water from which the surface water level is measured.

Soil Horizon - A layer of soil or soil material approximately parallel to the land surface and differing from adjacent layers in physical, chemical, and biological properties or characteristics (e.g., color, structure, and texture).

Substrate - The surface beneath a wetland in which organisms grow or to which organisms are attached.

Stewardship (Land) - To care for and manage natural land in a way that maintains its ecological integrity for the benefit of present and future generations.

Swamp - A forested wetland.

Transpiration - The process in plants by which water is released into the gaseous environment (atmosphere).

Tree - A woody plant 5 inches or greater in diameter at breast height and 20 feet or taller.

Upland - Any area that does not qualify as a wetland because the associated hydrologic regime is not sufficiently wet to elicit development of vegetation, soil, and/or hydrologic characteristics associated with wetlands.

Wetland - An area that is inundated or saturated to the surface for a sufficient time to foster the growth of hydrophytic plants and/or the development of hydric soils.

Wetland Boundary - The point on the ground at which a shift from wetland to upland occurs.

Wetland Delineation - The process by which the boundaries of a particular wetland are defined.

Wetland Determination - The process by which an area is identified as a wetland or nonwetland.

Wetland Hydrology - In general terms, inundation or prolonged soil saturation for a duration sufficient to support wetland vegetation or foster the development of hydric soils (approximately 14 days or more during the growing season in the temperate zone).

Wetland Indicator Status - One of five categories which provide an estimate of the percentage of time a particular plant species would occur in a wetland.

Zone of influence - The area contiguous to a ditch, channel, or other drainage structure that is directly drained by it.

NATURAL RESOURCES AND ENVIRONMENTAL PROTECTION ACT
Act 451 of 1994

AN ACT to protect the environment and natural resources of the state; to codify, revise, consolidate, and classify laws relating to the environment and natural resources of the state; to regulate the discharge of certain substances into the environment; to regulate the use of certain lands, waters, and other natural resources of the state; to prescribe the powers and duties of certain state and local agencies and officials; to provide for certain charges, fees, and assessments; to prescribe penalties and provide remedies; to repeal certain parts of this act on a specific date; and to repeal certain acts and parts of acts.

History: 1994, Act 451, Eff. Mar. 30, 1994.

The People of the State of Michigan enact:

ARTICLE I GENERAL PROVISIONS

PART 1 SHORT TITLE AND SAVINGS CLAUSES

324.101 Short title.
Sec. 101. This act shall be known and may be cited as the "natural resources and environmental protection act".
History: 1994, Act 451, Eff. Mar. 30, 1995.

324.102 Repeal of statute; effect.
Sec. 102. The repeal of any statute by this act does not relinquish any penalty, forfeiture, or liability, whether criminal or civil in nature, and such statute shall be treated as still remaining in force as necessary for the purpose of instituting or sustaining any proper action or prosecution for the enforcement of the penalty, forfeiture, or liability.
History: 1994, Act 451, Eff. Mar. 30, 1995.

324.103 Heading or title; effect.
Sec. 103. A heading or title of an article, chapter, part, or subpart of this act shall not be considered as a part of this act or be used to construe the act more broadly or narrowly than the text of the sections of the act would indicate, but shall be considered as inserted for the convenience of the users of this act.
History: 1994, Act 451, Eff. Mar. 30, 1995.

324.104 Members of predecessor agency; powers.
Sec. 104. When a board, commission, committee, council, or other agency created by or pursuant to this act was preceded by an agency with the same or similar name and functions, members of the predecessor agency shall continue in office for the duration of the terms of office for which they were appointed and with the new members appointed shall constitute the new agency. Members shall be appointed under this act only as terms of the former members expire or vacancies occur. Members of the predecessor agency may be appointed to the new agency to succeed themselves subject to the limits for the total period of service set forth in this act.
History: 1994, Act 451, Eff. Mar. 30, 1995.

324.105 Existing rules; effect.
Sec. 105. When the department or other agency is directed to promulgate rules by this act and rules exist on the date the requirement to promulgate rules takes effect, which rules the department or agency believes adequately cover the matter, the department or agency may determine that new rules are not required or may delay the promulgation of new rules until the department or agency considers it advisable.
History: 1994, Act 451, Eff. Mar. 30, 1995.

PART 303
WETLANDS PROTECTION

324.30301 Definitions.
Sec. 30301. As used in this part:

(a) "Fill material" means soil, rocks, sand, waste of any kind, or any other material that displaces soil or water or reduces water retention potential.

(b) "Minor drainage" includes ditching and tiling for the removal of excess soil moisture incidental to the planting, cultivating, protecting, or harvesting of crops or improving the productivity of land in established use for agriculture, horticulture, silviculture, or lumbering.

(c) "Person" means an individual, sole proprietorship, partnership, corporation, association, municipality, this state, and instrumentality or agency of this state, the federal government, or an instrumentality or agency of the federal government, or other legal entity.

(d) "Wetland" means land characterized by the presence of water at a frequency and duration sufficient to support, and that under normal circumstances does support, wetland vegetation or aquatic life, and is commonly referred to as a bog, swamp, or marsh and which is any of the following:

(i) Contiguous to the Great Lakes or Lake St. Clair, an inland lake or pond, or a river or stream.

(ii) Not contiguous to the Great Lakes, an inland lake or pond, or a river or stream; and more than 5 acres in size; except this subparagraph shall not be of effect, except for the purpose of inventorying, in counties of less than 100,000 population until the department certifies to the commission it has substantially completed its inventory of wetlands in that county.

(iii) Not contiguous to the Great Lakes, an inland lake or pond, or a river or stream; and 5 acres or less in size if the department determines that protection of the area is essential to the preservation of the natural resources of the state from pollution, impairment, or destruction and the department has so notified the owner; except this subparagraph may be utilized regardless of wetland size in a county in which subparagraph (ii) is of no effect, except for the purpose of inventorying, at the time.
History: Add. 1995, Act 59, Imd. Eff. May 24, 1995.

324.30302 Legislative findings; criteria to be considered in administration of part.
Sec. 30302. (1) The legislature finds that:

(a) Wetland conservation is a matter of state concern since a wetland of 1 county may be affected by acts on a river, lake, stream, or wetland of other counties.

(b) A loss of a wetland may deprive the people of the state of some or all of the following benefits to be derived from the wetland:

(i) Flood and storm control by the hydrologic absorption and storage capacity of the wetland.

(ii) Wildlife habitat by providing breeding, nesting, and feeding grounds and cover for many forms of wildlife, waterfowl, including migratory waterfowl, and rare, threatened, or endangered wildlife species.

(iii) Protection of subsurface water resources and provision of valuable watersheds and recharging ground water supplies.

(iv) Pollution treatment by serving as a biological and chemical oxidation basin.

324.106 Orders; effect.
Sec. 106. Except as otherwise provided by law, this act does not repeal or alter the content or effect of orders that were issued pursuant to an act that is repealed by this act and codified as a part of this act.
History: 1994, Act 451, Eff. Mar. 30, 1995.

324.107 Editorial changes; effect; intent.
Sec. 107. It is the intention of the legislature that editorial changes in the language of statutes codified as parts within this act not be construed as changes to the meanings of those statutes.
History: Add. 1995, Act 60, Imd. Eff. May 24, 1995.

PART 3 DEFINITIONS

324.301 Definitions.
Sec. 301. Except as otherwise defined in this act, as used in this act:

(a) "Commission" means the commission of natural resources.

(b) "Department" means the director of the department of natural resources or his or her designee to whom the director delegates a power or duty by written instrument.

(c) "Department of natural resources" means the principal state department created in section 501.

(d) "Director" means the director of the department of natural resources.

(e) "Local unit of government" means a municipality or county.

(f) "Municipality" means a city, village, or township.

(g) "Person" means an individual, partnership, corporation, association, governmental entity, or other legal entity.

(h) "Public domain" means all land owned by the state or land deeded to the state under state law.

(i) "Rule" means a rule promulgated pursuant to the administrative procedures act of 1969, Act No. 306 of the Public Acts of 1969, being sections 24.201 to 24.328 of the Michigan Compiled Laws.
History: 1994, Act 451, Eff. Mar. 30, 1995.

(v) Erosion control by serving as a sedimentation area and filtering basin, absorbing silt and organic matter.

(vi) Sources of nutrients in water food cycles and nursery grounds and sanctuaries for fish.

(c) Wetlands are valuable as an agricultural resource for the production of food and fiber, including certain crops which may only be grown on sites developed from wetland.

(d) That the extraction and processing of nonfuel minerals may necessitate the use of wetland, if it is determined pursuant to section 30311 that the proposed activity is dependent upon being located in the wetland and that a prudent and feasible alternative does not exist.

(2) In the administration of this part, the department shall consider the criteria provided in subsection (1).
History: Add. 1995, Act 59, Imd. Eff. May 24, 1995.

324.30303 Studies regarding wetland resources; contracts; study as public record for distribution at cost.

Sec. 30303. The department may enter into an agreement to make contracts with the federal government, other state agencies, local units of government, private agencies, or persons for the purposes of making studies for the efficient preservation, management, protection, and use of wetland resources. A study shall be available as a public record for distribution at cost as provided in section 4 of the freedom of information act, Act No. 442 of the Public Acts of 1976, being section 15.234 of the Michigan Compiled Laws.
History: Add. 1995, Act 59, Imd. Eff. May 24, 1995.

324.30304 Prohibited activities.

Sec. 30304. Except as otherwise provided by this part or by a permit obtained from the department under sections 30306 to 30314, a person shall not do any of the following:

(a) Deposit or permit the placing of fill material in a wetland.

(b) Dredge, remove, or permit the removal of soil or minerals from a wetland.

(c) Construct, operate, or maintain any use or development in a wetland.

(d) Drain surface water from a wetland.
History: Add. 1995, Act 59, Imd. Eff. May 24, 1995.

324.30305 Activities not requiring permit under part; uses not requiring permit; additional permit not required for project involving discharge of certain fill material.

Sec. 30305. (1) Activities which require a permit under part 325 or part 301 do not require a permit under this part.

(2) The following uses are allowed in a wetland without a permit subject to other laws of this state and the owner's regulation:

(a) Fishing, trapping, or hunting.

(b) Swimming or boating.

(c) Hiking.

(d) Grazing of animals.

(e) Farming, horticulture, silviculture, lumbering, and ranching activities, including plowing, irrigation, irrigation ditching, seeding, cultivating, minor drainage, harvesting for the production of food, fiber, and forest products, or upland soil and water conservation practices. Wetland altered under this subsection shall not be used for a purpose other than a purpose described in this subsection without a permit from the department.

(f) Maintenance or operation of serviceable structures in existence on October 1, 1980 or constructed pursuant to this part or former Act No. 203 of the Public Acts of 1979.

(g) Construction or maintenance of farm or stock ponds.

(h) Maintenance, operation, or improvement which includes straightening, widening, or deepening of the following which is necessary for the production or harvesting of agricultural products:

(i) An existing private agricultural drain.

(ii) That portion of a drain legally established pursuant to the drain code of 1956, Act No. 40 of the Public Acts of 1956, being sections 280.1 to 280.630 of the Michigan Compiled Laws, which has been constructed or improved for drainage purposes.

(iii) A drain constructed pursuant to other provisions of this part or former Act No. 203 of the Public Acts of 1979.

(i) Construction or maintenance of farm roads, forest roads, or temporary roads for moving mining or forestry equipment, if the roads are constructed and maintained in a manner to assure that any adverse effect on the wetland will be otherwise minimized.

(j) Drainage necessary for the production and harvesting of agricultural products if the wetland is owned by a person who is engaged in commercial farming and the land is to be used for the production and harvesting of agricultural products. Except as otherwise provided in this part, wetland improved under this subdivision after October 1, 1980 shall not be used for nonfarming purposes without a permit from the department. This subdivision shall not apply to a wetland which is contiguous to a lake or stream, or to a tributary of a lake or stream, or to a wetland that the department has determined by clear and convincing evidence to be a wetland that is necessary to be preserved for the public interest, in which case a permit is required.

(k) Maintenance or improvement of public streets, highways, or roads, within the right-of-way and in such a manner as to assure that any adverse effect on the wetland will be otherwise minimized. Maintenance or improvement does not include adding extra lanes, increasing the right-of-way, or deviating from the existing location of the street, highway, or road.

(l) Maintenance, repair, or operation of gas or oil pipelines and construction of gas or oil pipelines having a diameter of 6 inches or less, if the pipelines are constructed, maintained, or repaired in a manner to assure that any adverse effect on the wetland will be otherwise minimized.

(m) Maintenance, repair, or operation of electric transmission and distribution power lines and construction of distribution power lines, if the distribution power lines are constructed, maintained, or repaired in a manner to assure that any adverse effect on the wetland will be otherwise minimized.

(n) Operation or maintenance, including reconstruction of recently damaged parts, of serviceable dikes and levees in existence on October 1, 1980 or constructed pursuant to this part or former Act No. 203 of the Public Acts of 1979.

(o) Construction of iron and copper mining tailings basins and water storage areas.

(3) After October 1, 1980 but immediately prior to the approval of a state program under section 404 of title IV of the federal water pollution control act, chapter 758, 86 Stat. 884, 33 U.S.C. 1344, where a project solely involves the discharge of fill material subject to the individual permit requirements of section 404 of title IV of the federal water pollution control act, an additional permit is not required by this part.

History: Add. 1995, Act 59, Imd. Eff. May 24, 1995.

324.30306 Permit for use or development listed in § 324.30304; filing, form, and contents of application; fee; exemption; proposed use or development as single permit application.

Sec. 30306. (1) Except as provided in section 30307(4), to obtain a permit for a use or development listed in section 30304, the person desiring the permit shall file an application with the department on a form provided by this the department accompanied by a fee of $25.00. A person who has a permit for the particular activity under part 301 or part 615 does not need to pay the fee prescribed by this subsection. The application shall include all of the following:

(a) The person's name and address.

(b) The location of the wetland.

(c) A description of the wetland on which the use or development is to be made.

(d) A statement describing the proposed use or development.

(e) The wetland owner's name and address.

(f) An environmental assessment, on a form supplied by the department, of the proposed use or development if requested by the department, which assessment shall include the effects upon wetland benefits and the effects upon the water quality, flow, and levels, and the wildlife, fish, and vegetation within a contiguous lake, river, or stream.

(2) For the purposes of subsection (1), a proposed use or development of a wetland shall be considered as a single permit application under this part if the scope, extent, and purpose of a use or development are made known at the time of the application for the permit.

History: Add. 1995, Act 59, Imd. Eff. May 24, 1995.

324.30307 Hearing; location; notice; approval or disapproval of permit application; notice of and reasons for denial or modifications; conditions; appeal; legal action; request and fee for notification of pending permit applications; biweekly list of applications; effect of ordinance regulating wetlands; review of permit application by local unit of government; effect of failure to approve or disapprove within time period; recommendations; notice of permit issuance.

Sec. 30307. (1) Within 60 days after receipt of the completed application and fee, the department may hold a hearing. If a hearing is held, it shall be held in the county where the wetland on which the permit is to apply is located. Notice of the hearing shall be made in the same manner as for the promulgation of rules under the administrative procedures act of 1969, Act No. 306 of the Public Acts of 1969, being sections 24.201 to 24.328 of the Michigan Compiled Laws. The department may approve or disapprove a permit application without a public hearing unless a person requests a hearing in writing within 20 days after the mailing of notification of the permit application as required by subsection (3) or unless the department determines that the permit application is of significant impact to warrant a public hearing.

(2) If a hearing is not held, the department shall approve or disapprove the permit application within 90 days after the completed permit application is filed with the department. If a hearing is held, the department shall approve or disapprove the permit application within 90 days after the conclusion of the hearing. The department may approve a permit application, request modifications in the application, or deny the permit application. If the department approves the permit application, the department shall prepare and send the permit to the applicant. If the department denies, or requests a modification of, the permit application, the department shall send notice of the denial or modification request and the reasons for the denial or the modifications requested to the applicant. Department approval may include the issuance of a permit containing conditions necessary for compliance with this part. If the department does not approve or disapprove the permit application within the time provided by this subsection, the permit application shall be considered approved, and the department shall be considered to have made the determinations required by section 30311. The action taken by the department may be appealed pursuant to Act No. 306 of the Public Acts of 1969. A property owner may, after exhaustion of administrative remedies, bring appropriate legal action in a court of competent jurisdiction.

(3) A person who desires notification of pending permit applications may make a written request to the department accompanied by an annual fee of $25.00, which shall be credited to the general fund of the state. The department shall prepare a biweekly list of the applications made during the previous 2 weeks and shall promptly mail copies of the list for the remainder of the calendar year to the persons who requested notice. The biweekly list shall state the name and address of each applicant, the location of the wetland in the proposed use or development, including the size of both the proposed use or development and of the wetland affected, and a summary statement of the purpose of the use or development.

(4) A local unit of government may regulate wetland within its boundaries, by ordinance, only as provided under this part. This subsection is supplemental to the existing authority of a local unit of government. An ordinance adopted by a local unit of government pursuant to this subsection shall comply with all of the following:

(a) The ordinance shall not provide a different definition of wetland than is provided in this part, except that a wetland ordinance may regulate wetland of less than 5 acres in size.

(b) If the ordinance regulates wetland that is smaller than 2 acres in size, the ordinance shall comply with section 30309.

(c) The ordinance shall comply with sections 30308 and 30310.

(d) The ordinance shall not require a permit for uses that are authorized without a permit under section 30305, and shall otherwise comply with this part.

(5) Each local unit of government that adopts an ordinance regulating wetlands under subsection (4) shall notify the department.

(6) A local unit of government that adopts an ordinance regulating wetlands shall use an application form supplied by the department, and each person applying for a permit shall make application directly to the local unit of government. Upon receipt, the local unit of government shall forward a copy of each application to the department. The department shall begin reviewing the application as provided in this part. The local unit of government shall review the application pursuant to its ordinance and shall modify, approve, or deny the application within 90 days after receipt. If a municipality does not approve or disapprove the permit application within the time period provided by this subsection, the permit application shall be considered approved, and the municipality shall be considered to have made the determinations as listed in section 30311. The denial of a permit shall be accompanied by a written statement of all reasons for denial. The failure to supply complete information with a permit application may be reason for denial of a permit. The department shall inform any interested person whether or not a local unit of government has an ordinance regulating wetlands. If the department receives an application with respect to a wetland which is located in a local unit of government which has an ordinance regulating wetlands, the department immediately shall forward the application to the local unit of government, which shall modify, deny, or approve the application under this subsection. The local unit of government shall notify the department of its decision. The department shall proceed as provided in this part.

(7) If a local unit of government does not have an ordinance regulating wetlands, the department shall promptly send a copy of the permit application to the local unit of government where the wetland is located. The local unit of government may review the application; may hold a hearing on the application; and may recommend approval, modification, or denial of the application to the department. The recommendations of the local unit of government

shall be made and returned to the department within 45 days after the local unit of government's receipt of the permit application. The department shall approve, modify, or deny the application as provided in this part.

(8) In addition to the requirements of subsection (7), the department shall notify the local unit of government that the department has issued a permit under this part within the jurisdiction of that local unit of government within 15 days of issuance of the permit. The department shall enclose a copy of the permit with the notice.

History: Add. 1995, Act 59, Imd. Eff. May 24, 1995.—Am. 1995, Act 103, Imd. Eff. June 23, 1995.

324.30308 Adoption of wetlands ordinance by local unit of government; availability of wetland inventory; completion of inventory map; notice; enforceable presumptions not created; processing wetland use applications.

Sec. 30308. (1) Prior to the effective date of an ordinance authorized under section 30307(4), a local unit of government that wishes to adopt such an ordinance shall complete and make available to the public at a reasonable cost an inventory of all wetland within the local unit of government, except that a local unit of government located in a county that has a population of less than 100,000 is not required to include public lands on its map. A local unit of government shall make a draft of the inventory map available to the public, shall provide for public notice and comment opportunity prior to finalizing the inventory map, and shall respond in writing to written comments received by the local unit of government regarding the contents of the inventory. A local unit of government that has a wetland ordinance on December 18, 1992 has until June 18, 1994 to complete an inventory map and to otherwise comply with this part, or the local unit of government shall not continue to enforce that ordinance. Upon completion of an inventory map or upon a subsequent amendment of an inventory map, the local unit of government shall notify each record owner of property on the property tax roll of the local unit of government that the inventory maps exist or have been amended, where the maps may be reviewed, that the owner's property may be designated as a wetland on the inventory map, and that the local unit of government has an ordinance regulating wetland. The notice shall also inform the property owner that the inventory map does not necessarily include all of the wetlands within the local unit of government that may be subject to the wetland ordinance. The notice may be given by including the required information with the annual notice of the property owner's property tax assessment. A wetland inventory map does not create any legally enforceable presumptions regarding whether property that is or is not included on the inventory map is or is not a wetland.

(2) A local unit of government that adopts a wetland ordinance shall process wetland use applications in a manner that ensures that the same entity makes decisions on site plans, plats, and related matters, and wetland determinations, and that the applicant is not required to submit to a hearing on the application before more than 1 local unit of government decision making body. This requirement does not apply to either of the following:

(a) A preliminary review by a planning department, planning consultant, or planning commission, prior to submittal to the decision making body if required by an ordinance.

(b) An appeal process that is provided for appeal to the legislative body or other body designated to hear appeals.

History: Add. 1995, Act 59, Imd. Eff. May 24, 1995.

324.30309 Regulation by local unit of government of wetland less than 2 acres; permit application; determination.

Sec. 30309. A local unit of government that has adopted an ordinance under section 30307(4) that regulates wetland within its jurisdiction that is less than 2 acres in size shall comply with this section. Upon application for a wetland use permit in a wetland that is less than 2 acres in size, the local unit of government shall approve the permit unless the local unit of government determines that the wetland is essential to the preservation of the natural resources of the local unit of government and provides these findings, in writing, to the permit applicant stating the reasons for this determination. In making this determination, the local unit of government must find that 1 or more of the following exist at the particular site:

(a) The site supports state or federal endangered or threatened plants, fish, or wildlife appearing on a list specified in section 36505.

(b) The site represents what is identified as a locally rare or unique ecosystem.

(c) The site supports plants or animals of an identified local importance.

(d) The site provides groundwater recharge documented by a public agency.

(e) The site provides flood and storm control by the hydrologic absorption and storage capacity of the wetland.

(f) The site provides wildlife habitat by providing breeding, nesting, or feeding grounds or cover for forms of wildlife, waterfowl, including migratory waterfowl, and rare, threatened, or endangered wildlife species.

(g) The site provides protection of subsurface water resources and provision of valuable watersheds and recharging groundwater supplies.

(h) The site provides pollution treatment by serving as a biological and chemical oxidation basin.

(i) The site provides erosion control by serving as a sedimentation area and filtering basin, absorbing silt and organic matter.

(j) The site provides sources of nutrients in water food cycles and nursery grounds and sanctuaries for fish.

History: Add. 1995, Act 59, Imd. Eff. May 24, 1995.

324.30310 Regulation by local unit of government of wetland less than 2 acres; revaluation for assessment purposes; protest and appeal; judicial review; right to initiate proceedings not limited by section.

Sec. 30310. (1) A local unit of government that adopts an ordinance authorized under section 30307(4) shall include in the ordinance a provision that allows a landowner to request a revaluation of the affected property for assessment purposes to determine its fair market value under the use restriction if a permit is denied by a local unit of government for a proposed wetland use. A landowner who is aggrieved by a determination, action, or inaction under this subsection may protest and appeal that determination, action, or inaction pursuant to the general property tax act, Act No. 206 of the Public Acts of 1893, being sections 211.1 to 211.157 of the Michigan Compiled Laws.

(2) If a permit applicant is aggrieved by a determination, action, or inaction by the local unit of government regarding the issuance of a permit, that person may seek judicial review in the same manner as provided in the administrative procedures act of 1969, Act No. 306 of the Public Acts of 1969, being sections 24.201 to 24.328 of the Michigan Compiled Laws.

(3) This section does not limit the right of a wetland owner to institute proceedings in any circuit of the circuit court of the state against any person when necessary to protect the wetland owner's rights.

History: Add. 1995, Act 59, Imd. Eff. May 24, 1995.

324.30311 Permit for activity listed in § 324.30304; approval conditioned on certain determinations; criteria; findings of necessity; criteria for determining unacceptable disruption to aquatic resources; additional showing.

Sec. 30311. (1) A permit for an activity listed in section 30304 shall not be approved unless the department determines that the issuance of a permit is in the public interest, that the permit is necessary to realize the benefits derived from the activity, and that the activity is otherwise lawful.

(2) In determining whether the activity is in the public interest, the benefit which reasonably may be expected to accrue from the proposal shall be balanced against the reasonably foreseeable detriments of the activity. The decision shall reflect the national and state concern for the protection of natural resources from pollution, impairment, and destruction. The following general criteria shall be considered:

(a) The relative extent of the public and private need for the proposed activity.

(b) The availability of feasible and prudent alternative locations and methods to accomplish the expected benefits from the activity.

(c) The extent and permanence of the beneficial or detrimental effects that the proposed activity may have on the public and private uses to which the area is suited, including the benefits the wetland provides.

(d) The probable impact of each proposal in relation to the cumulative effect created by other existing and anticipated activities in the watershed.

(e) The probable impact on recognized historic, cultural, scenic, ecological, or recreational values and on the public health or fish or wildlife.

(f) The size of the wetland being considered.

(g) The amount of remaining wetland in the general area.

(h) Proximity to any waterway.

(i) Economic value, both public and private, of the proposed land change to the general area.

(3) In considering a permit application, the department shall give serious consideration to findings of necessity for the proposed activity which have been made by other state agencies.

(4) A permit shall not be issued unless it is shown that an unacceptable disruption will not result to the aquatic resources. In determining whether a disruption to the aquatic resources is unacceptable, the criteria set forth in section 30302 and subsection (2) shall be considered. A permit shall not be issued unless the applicant also shows either of the following:

(a) The proposed activity is primarily dependent upon being located in the wetland.

(b) A feasible and prudent alternative does not exist.
History: Add 1995, Act 59, Imd. Eff. May 24, 1995.

324.30312 General permit for category of activities; notice and public hearing; determinations; requirements and standards; conditions; time for completion or termination of construction, development, or use; duration of general permit.

Sec. 30312. (1) The department, after notice and opportunity for a public hearing, may issue general permits on a state or county basis for a category of activities if the department determines that the activities are similar in nature, will cause only minimal adverse environmental effects when performed separately, and will have only minimal cumulative adverse effect on the environment. A general permit issued under this subsection shall be based on the requirements of this part and the rules promulgated under this part and shall apply to an activity authorized by the general permit.

(2) The department may impose conditions on a permit for a use or development if the conditions are designed to remove an impairment to the wetland benefits, to mitigate the impact of a discharge of fill material, or to otherwise improve the water quality.

(3) The department may establish a reasonable time when the construction, development, or use is to be completed or terminated. A general permit shall not be valid for more than 5 years.
History: Add 1995, Act 59, Imd. Eff. May 24, 1995.

324.30313 Grounds for revocation or modification of general permit; grounds for termination or modification for cause of general permit.

Sec. 30313. (1) A general permit may be revoked or modified if, after opportunity for a public hearing or a contested case hearing under the administrative procedures act of 1969, Act No. 306 of the Public Acts of 1969, being sections 24.201 to 24.328 of the Michigan Compiled Laws, the department determines that the activities authorized by the general permit have an adverse impact on the environment or the activities would be more appropriately authorized by an individual permit.

(2) A permit may be terminated or modified for cause, including:

(a) A violation of a condition of the permit.

(b) Obtaining a permit by misrepresentation or failure to fully disclose relevant facts.

(c) A change in a condition that requires a temporary or permanent change in the activity.
History: Add 1995, Act 59, Imd. Eff. May 24, 1995.

324.30314 Information required to obtain compliance with part; entering on premises.

Sec. 30314. (1) The department shall require the holder of a permit to provide information the department reasonably requires to obtain compliance with this part.

(2) Upon reasonable cause or obtaining a search warrant, the department may enter on, upon, or through the premises on which an activity listed in section 30304 is located or on which information required to be maintained under subsection (1) is located.
History: Add 1995, Act 59, Imd. Eff. May 24, 1995.

324.30315 Violation; order requiring compliance; civil action.

Sec. 30315. (1) If, on the basis of information available to the department, the department finds that a person is in violation of this part or a condition set forth in a permit issued under section 30311 or 30312, the department shall issue an order requiring the person to comply with the prohibitions or conditions or the department shall request the attorney general to bring a civil action under section 30316(1).

(2) An order issued under subsection (1) shall state with reasonable specificity the nature of the violation and shall specify a time for compliance, not to exceed 30 days, which the department determines is reasonable, taking into account the seriousness of the violation and good faith efforts to comply with applicable requirements.
History: Add 1995, Act 59, Imd. Eff. May 24, 1995.

324.30316 Civil action; commencement; request; venue; jurisdiction; violations; penalties; restoration of wetland.

Sec. 30316. (1) The attorney general may commence a civil action for appropriate relief, including injunctive relief upon request of the department under section 30315(1). An action under this subsection may be brought in the circuit court for the county of Ingham or for a county in which the defendant is located, resides, or is doing business. The court has jurisdiction to restrain the violation and to require compliance with this part. In addition to any other relief granted under this section, the court may impose a civil fine of not more than $10,000.00 per day of violation. A person who violates an order of the court is subject to a civil fine not to exceed $10,000.00 for each day of violation.

(2) A person who violates this part is guilty of a misdemeanor, punishable by a fine of not more than $2,500.00.

(3) A person who willfully or recklessly violates a condition or limitation in a permit issued by the department under this part, or a corporate officer who has knowledge of or is responsible for a violation, is guilty of a misdemeanor, punishable by a fine of not less than $2,500.00 nor more than $25,000.00 per day of violation, or by imprisonment for not more than 1 year, or both. A person who violates this section a second or subsequent time is

guilty of a felony, punishable by a fine of not more than $50,000.00 for each day of violation, or by imprisonment for not more than 2 years, or both.

(4) In addition to the penalties provided under subsections (1), (2), and (3), the court may order a person who violates this part to restore as nearly as possible the wetland that was affected by the violation to its original condition immediately before the violation. The restoration may include the removal of fill material deposited in the wetland or the replacement of soil, sand, or minerals.

History: Add. 1995, Act 59 Imd. Eff. May 24, 1995.

324.30317 Disposition of fees and civil fines.

Sec. 30317. The fees and civil fines collected under this part shall be deposited in the general fund of the state. Other than criminal fines, funds collected by a local unit of government under an ordinance authorized under section 30307(4) shall be deposited in the general fund of the local unit of government.

History: Add. 1995, Act 59 Imd. Eff. May 24, 1995.

324.30318 Revaluation of property for assessment purposes.

Sec. 30318. If a permit is denied for a proposed wetland activity, the landowner may request a revaluation of the affected property for assessment purposes to determine its fair market value under the use restriction.

History: Add. 1995, Act 59, Imd. Eff. May 24, 1995.

324.30319 Rules; hearing; judicial review; proceedings to protect wetland owner's rights.

Sec. 30319. (1) The department shall promulgate and enforce rules to implement this part.

(2) If a person is aggrieved by any action or inaction of the department, the person may request a formal hearing on the matter involved. The hearing shall be conducted by the department pursuant to the administrative procedures act of 1969, Act No. 306 of the Public Acts of 1969, being sections 24.201 to 24.328 of the Michigan Compiled Laws.

(3) A determination, action, or inaction by the department following the hearing is subject to judicial review as provided in Act No. 306 of the Public Acts of 1969.

(4) This section does not limit the right of a wetland owner to institute proceedings in any circuit of the circuit court of the state against any person when necessary to protect the wetland owner's rights.

History: Add. 1995, Act 55, Imd. Eff. May 24, 1995.

324.30320 Inventories of wetland; use; updating; maps, ground surveys, and descriptions as public documents; availability and cost of aerial photographs and satellite telemetry data reproduction to county register of deeds.

Sec. 30320. (1) As inventories of wetland are completed, the inventories shall be used as 1 of the criteria by the department in issuing permits. The inventories shall be periodically updated. The maps, ground surveys, and descriptions of wetlands included in the inventories shall be submitted to the respective county register of deeds and shall become a public document available to review by any member of the public.

(2) Aerial photographs and satellite telemetry data reproductions shall be made available to the respective county register of deeds for cost as determined by the department.

History: Add. 1995, Act 55, Imd. Eff. May 24, 1995.

324.30321 Basis and filing of preliminary inventory of wetland; hearing in state planning and development region; notice; issuance and distribution of final inventory; legislators to receive inventories; inspection of property; written wetland determination; inventory not to delay implementation of part.

Sec. 30321. (1) The department shall make or cause to be made a preliminary inventory of all wetland in this state on a county by county basis and file the inventory with the agricultural extension office, register of deeds, and county clerk.

(2) At least 2 hearings shall be held in each state planning and development region created by Executive Directive No. 1973-1. The hearing shall be held by the department after publication and due notice so that interested parties may comment on the inventory. After the hearings, the department shall issue a final inventory which shall be sent and kept by the agricultural extension office, register of deeds, and county clerk. Legislators shall receive an inventory of a county or regional classification for their districts including both preliminary and final inventories unless the legislators request not to receive the materials.

(3) Before an inventory is made of a county, interested persons may request the department to inspect property, and the department shall make a written wetland determination. The determination shall be made within a reasonable time after the request. Completion of the inventory shall not delay implementation of this part.

History: Add. 1995, Act 59, Imd. Eff. May 24, 1995.

324.30322 Notice to owners of record of change in status of property.

Sec. 30322. As wetland inventories are completed as specified in section 30321, owners of record as identified by the current property tax roll shall be notified of the possible change in the status of their property. Notification shall be printed on the next property tax bill mailed to property owners in the county. It shall contain information specifying that a wetland inventory has been completed and is on file with the agricultural extension office, register of deeds, and county clerk, and that property owners may be subject to regulation under this part.

History: Add. 1995, Act 59, Imd. Eff. May 24, 1995.

324.30323 Legal rights or authority not abrogated; action to determine if property taken without just compensation; court order; limitation on value of property.

Sec. 30323. (1) This part shall not be construed to abrogate rights or authority otherwise provided by law.

(2) For the purposes of determining if there has been a taking of property without just compensation under state law, an owner of property who has sought and been denied a permit from the state or from a local unit of government that adopts an ordinance pursuant to section 30307(4), who has been made subject to modifications or conditions in the permit under this part, or who has been made subject to the action or inaction of the department pursuant to this part or the action or inaction of a local unit of government that adopts an ordinance pursuant to section 30307(4) may file an action in a court of competent jurisdiction.

(3) If the court determines that an action of the department or a local unit of government pursuant to this part or an ordinance authorized pursuant to section 30307(4) constitutes a taking of the property of a person, then the court shall order the department or the local unit of government, at the department's or the local unit of government's option, as applicable, to do 1 or more of the following:

(a) Compensate the property owner for the full amount of the lost value.

(b) Purchase the property in the public interest as determined before its value was affected by this part or the local ordinance authorized under section 30307(4) or the action or inaction of the department pursuant to this part or the local unit of government pursuant to its ordinance.

(c) Modify its action or inaction with respect to the property so as to minimize the detrimental affect to the property's value.

(4) For the purposes of this section, the value of the property may not exceed that share of the state equalized valuation of the total parcel that the area in dispute occupies of the total parcel of land, multiplied by 2, as determined by an inspection of the most recent assessment roll of the township or city in which the parcel is located.

History: Add. 1995, Act 59, Imd. Eff. May 24, 1995.

ACT 203 OF PUBLIC ACTS OF 1979
REPLACED BY
THE NATURAL RESOURCES AND
ENVIRONMENTAL PROTECTION ACT
1994 PUBLIC ACT 451

DEPARTMENT OF NATURAL RESOURCES
LAND AND WATER MANAGEMENT DIVISION
WETLAND PROTECTION

(By authority conferred on the department of natural resources by section 17 of Act No. 203 of the Public Acts of 1979, being §281.717 of the Michigan Compiled Laws)

R 281.921   Definitions.

Rule 1. (1) As used in these rules:

(a) "Act" means Act No. 203 of the Public Acts of 1979, being §281.701 et seq. of the Michigan Compiled Laws.

(b) "Contiguous" means any of the following:

(i) A permanent surface water connection or other direct physical contact with an inland lake or pond, a river or stream, on of the Great Lakes, or Lake St. Clair.

(ii) A seasonal or intermittent direct surface water connection to an inland lake or pond, a river or stream, one of the Great Lakes, or Lake St. Clair.

(iii) A wetland is partially or entirely located within 500 feet of the ordinary high watermark of an inland lake or pond or a river or stream or is within 1,000 feet of the ordinary high watermark of one of the Great Lakes or Lake St. Clair, unless it is determined by the department, pursuant to R 281.924(4), that there is no surface water or groundwater connection to these waters.

(iv) Two or more areas of wetland separated only by barriers, such as dikes, roads, berms, or other similar features, but with any of the wetland areas contiguous under the criteria described in paragraph (i), (ii), or (iii) of this subdivision. The connecting waters of the Great Lakes, including the St. Mary's, St. Clair, and Detroit rivers, shall be considered part of the Great Lakes for purposes of this definition.

(c) "General permit" means a permit which, as authorized by section 10 of the act, is issued for categories of minor activities, as defined in subdivision (f) of this subrule.

(d) "Individual permit" means a permit which, as authorized by sections 7, 8, and 9 of the act, is issued for categories of activities that are not classified as minor.

(e) "Inland lake or pond, a river or stream" means any of the following:

(i) A river or stream which has definite banks, a bed, and visible evidence of a continued flow or continued occurrence of water.

(ii) A natural or permanent artificial inland lake or impoundment that has definite banks, a bed, and a surface area of water that is more than 5 acres. This does not include lakes constructed by excavating or diking dry land and maintained for the sole purpose of cooling or storing water and does not include lagoons used for treating polluted water.

(iii) A natural or permanent artificial pond that has permanent open water with a surface area that is more than 1 acre, but less than 5 acres. This does not include ponds constructed by excavating or diking dry land and maintained for the sole purpose of cooling or storing water and does not include lagoons used for treating polluted water.

(f) "Minor activities" means activities that are similar in nature, that will cause only minimal adverse environmental effects when performed separately, and that will have only minimal cumulative adverse effects on the environment.

(g) "Wetland vegetation" means plants that exhibit adaptations to allow, under normal conditions, germination or propagation and to allow growth with at least their root systems in water or saturated soil.

(2) As used in the act:

(a) "Electric distribution line" means underground lines below 30 kilovolts and lines supported by wood poles.

(b) "Electric transmission line" means those conductors and their necessary supporting or containing structures located outside of buildings that are used for transmitting a supply of electric energy, except those lines defined in subdivision (a) of this subrule.

(c) "Pipelines having a diameter of 6 inches or less" means a pipe which is equal to or less than what is commonly referred to as a 6-inch pipe and which has an actual measured outside diameter of less than 6.75 inches.

(3) Terms defined in the act have the same meanings when used in these rules.

R 281.922   Permit applications.

Rule 2. (1) An application for a permit shall be made on a form prescribed and provided by the department.

(2) An application for a permit shall not be deemed as received or filed until the department has received all information requested on the application form, the application fee, and other information authorized by the act and necessary to reach a decision. The period of granting or denying an application begins as soon as all such information and the application fee are received by the department.

(3) Application fees shall be submitted to the department with the initial submittal of an application form. The fee shall be paid by check, money order, or draft made payable to: "State of Michigan".

(4) An application may be considered to be withdrawn and the file for the application may be closed if an applicant fails to respond to any written inquiry or request from the department for information requested as a part of the application form within 30 days of the request or such longer period of time as needed by the applicant to provide the information agreed to, in writing, between the applicant and the department.

(5) Upon request, the department shall provide any person with a copy of a permit application and supporting documents consistent with all provisions of Act No. 442 of the Public Acts of 1976, as amended, being §15.231 et seq. of the Michigan Compiled Laws.

(6) Decisions reached by the department which deny or modify an application for a permit shall be supported by written documentation to the applicant based upon the applicable criteria contained in section 9 of the act. The department shall create a form based on the criteria from section 9 of the act to be completed and placed into each application file. When a proposed activity involves a coordinated review by federal agencies as provided for under the act and section 404 of title 4 of the clean water act of 1977, 33 U.S.C. §1344, the department shall prepare a fact sheet pursuant to 40 C.F.R. §124.8 (April 1, 1983) and 40 C.F.R. §233.39 (April 1, 1983) for inclusion in the application file.

R 281.923   Permits.

Rule 3. (1) An application for a proposed activity which is within a general permit category may be processed and issued by the department without the noticing or hearings specified under section 7, 8, and 9 of the act. The department may process, by public notice, an application which would normally qualify under a general permit category to allow more opportunity for public review and comment. Categories of minor activities will be established in the general permit in accordance with section 10 of the act. The factors set forth in sections 3 and 9 of the act shall be considered in determining whether such a permit is in the best interest of the public.

(2) Applications for activities that are not classified as minor shall be reviewed through the process prescribed under sections 7, 8, and 9 of the act. The department may issue an individual permit 21 days after the mailing of notification of the permit application if comments of nonobjection have been received from the

municipality, if a public hearing has not been requested, and if the proposed activities are otherwise in accordance with the act.

(3) If the department does not approve or disapprove the permit application within the time provided by section 8(2) of the act, the permit application shall be considered approved and the department shall be considered to have made the determination required by section 9 of the act.

(4) When a project involves activities regulated under Act No. 247 of the Public Acts of 1955, as amended, being 701 et seq. of the Michigan Compiled Laws, or Act No. 346 of the Public Acts of 1972, as amended, being 951 et seq. of the Michigan Compiled Laws, or the act, the applicant shall submit 1 application for all activities regulated under these acts. If a permit is issued, conditions shall reflect the requirements of all appropriate acts.

(5) A permit may be issued for a period extending until the end of the following calendar year. A permit may be issued for a longer period of time if agreed to, in writing, between the applicant and the department. Before a permit expires, extensions of time may be granted by the department upon receipt of a written request from the permit holder explaining why such an extension is needed to complete the project. Up to two 12-month extensions shall be granted if there is no change in the activity for which the permit was originally issued. Administrative fees shall not be required for such extensions.

(6) Any permit issued under the act does not obviate the necessity of receiving, when applicable, approval from other federal, state, and local government agencies.

(7) Any permit issued by the department under the act may be revoked or suspended, after notice and an opportunity for a hearing, for any of the following causes:

(a) A violation of a condition of the permit.

(b) Obtaining a permit by misrepresentation or failure to fully disclose relevant facts in the application.

(c) A change in a condition that requires a temporary or permanent change in the activity.

R 281.924 Wetland determinations.

Rule 4. (1) When performing wetland determinations, as required by section 19(3) of the act, the department shall utilize criteria consistent with the definition of "wetland" provided in section 2(g) of the act and shall provide a written response stating, to the legal landowner within 30 days of the on-site evaluation, whether the parcel contains wetland and the basis for that determination.

(2) When performing wetland determinations, the department shall rely on visible evidence that the existence of the area is above, at, or near the surface of the area to verify the existence of a wetland. Under normal circumstances, the frequency and duration of water that is necessary to determine an area to be a wetland will be reflected in the vegetation or aquatic life present within the area being considered. A wetland that has not been recently or severely disturbed will contain a predominance, not just an occurrence, of wetland vegetation or aquatic life. Where there is a predominance of wetland vegetation, and no direct visible evidence that water is, or has been, at or above the surface, the department shall use the following characteristics of the soils or substrate to verify the existence of a wetland:

(a) The presence of a soil that is saturated, flooded, or ponded long enough during the growing season to develop anaerobic conditions in the upper part of the soil that favor the growth and regeneration of wetland vegetation.

(b) Physical or chemical characteristics of a soil column which provide evidence of the current and recent degree of saturation or inundation. Characteristics, such as gleying, low chroma mottling, or chemically demonstrated anaerobic conditions, can be utilized to identify the current and recent depth and fluctuation of the water table or inundation.

(3) If the department makes a determination that a wetland otherwise outside of the jurisdiction of the act is essential to the preservation of the natural resources of the state under section 2(g)(iii) of the act, it shall provide such findings, in writing, to the legal landowner stating the reasons for this determination. In making such a determination, 1 or more of the following functions shall apply to a particular site:

(a) It supports state or federal endangered or threatened plants, fish, or wildlife appearing on a list specified in section 6 of Act No. 203 of the Public Acts of 1974, being 226 of the Michigan Compiled Laws.

(b) It represents what the department has identified as a rare or unique ecosystem.

(c) It supports plants or animals of an identified regional importance.

(d) It provides groundwater recharge documented by a public agency.

(4) Upon the request of a property owner or his or her agent, the department shall determine if there is no surface or groundwater connection that meets the definition of contiguous under R 281.921(1)(b)(iii). The determination shall be made in writing and shall be provided to the property owner or agent within a reasonable period of time after receipt of the request.

R 281.925 Mitigation.

Rule 5. (1) As authorized by section 10(2) of the act, the department may impose conditions on a permit for a use or development if the conditions are designed to remove an impairment to the wetland benefits, to mitigate the impact of a discharge of fill material, or otherwise improve the water quality.

(2) The department shall consider a mitigation plan if submitted by the applicant and may incorporate the mitigation actions as permit conditions for the improvement of the existing wetland resources or the creation of a new wetland resource to offset wetland resource losses resulting from the proposed project. If agreed to by the applicant, financial assurances may be required to ensure that mitigation is accomplished as specified by the permit conditions. The department shall, when requested by the applicant, meet with the applicant to review the applicant's mitigation plan.

(3) In developing conditions to mitigate impacts, the department shall consider mitigation to apply only to unavoidable impacts that are otherwise permittable utilizing the criteria under sections 3 and 9 of the act. Mitigation shall not be considered when it is feasible and prudent to avoid impacts or when the impacts would be otherwise prohibited under the act.

(4) When considering mitigation proposals, the department shall make all of the following determinations:

(a) That all feasible and prudent efforts have been made to avoid the loss of wetland resource values.

(b) That all practical means have been considered to minimize impacts.

(c) That it is practical to replace the wetland resource values which will be unavoidably impacted.

(5) If the department determines that it is practical to replace the wetland resource values which will be unavoidably impacted, the department shall consider all of the following criteria when reviewing an applicant's mitigation proposal:

(a) Mitigation shall be provided on-site where practical and beneficial to the wetland resources.

(b) When subdivision (a) of this subrule does not apply, mitigation shall be provided in the immediate vicinity of the permitted activity where practical and beneficial to the wetland resources. When possible, this means within the same watershed and municipality as the location of the proposed project.

(c) Only when it has been determined that subdivisions (a) and (b) of this subrule are inappropriate and impractical shall mitigation be considered elsewhere.

(d) Any proposal shall assure that, upon completion, there will be no net loss to the wetland resources.

(e) The proposal shall give consideration to replacement of the predominant functional values lost within the impacted wetland.

(6) Except where a mitigation plan is to occur on state or federally owned property or where the mitigation is to occur in the same municipality where the project is proposed, the municipality where the proposed mitigation site is located shall be given notice and an opportunity to comment in writing to the department on the proposed mitigation plan before a permit is issued.

(7) Any mitigation activity shall be completed before initiation of other permitted activities, unless a phased concurrent schedule can be agreed upon between the department and the applicant.

(8) Monitoring to establish documentation of the functional performance of the mitigation may be required as permit conditions, as well as necessary corrective actions required, to deliver the wetland resource values identified.

(9) Mitigation, by replacement of lost wetland resources, shall not be required if an activity is authorized and permitted under the authority of a general permit issued under section 10(1) of the act.

References

In an effort to enhance readability, the text contains no direct citations or footnotes. However, there were many resources that provided valuable background information either directly or indirectly for the content of this book. These resources are included below. This list of references can also serve as a bibliography for your further reading.

Barnes, B.V. and W.H. Wagner, Jr. *Michigan Trees: A Guide to the Trees of Michigan and the Great Lakes Region* University of Michigan, Ann Arbor, MI 1981

Brooks, R.P., D.A. Devlin, J. Hassinger. *Wetlands and Wildlife* Pennsylvania State University, University Park, PA 1993

Burke, David G. et. al. *Protecting Nontidal Wetlands* American Planning Association, Washington, D.C. 1988

Chabot, Amy. "Preliminary Results from the Marsh Monitoring Program in 1995" in Volume 7, Number 1 *Great Lakes Wetlands* edited by Wilfred Cwikiel. Tip of the Mitt Watershed Council, Conway, MI 1996

Cwikiel, Wilfred. *Michigan Wetlands: Yours to Protect (Second Edition)* Tip of the Mitt Watershed Council, Conway, MI 1992

Cowardin, Lewis M. et. al. *Classification of Wetlands and Deepwater Habitats of the United States* U.S. Department of Interior, U.S. Fish and Wildlife Services, Office of Biological Services, Washington, D.C. 1979

Dahl, T.E. *Wetlands Losses in the United States 1780 to 1980's* U.S. Department of the Interior, Fish and Wildlife Service, Washington, D.C. 1990

Dean, Lillian F. *Protecting Wetlands at the Local Level: Options for Southeast Michigan Communities* Rouge River Watershed Council, Detroit, MI 1991

East Michigan Environmental Action Council. *A Guide to Michigan's Watercourse and Wetland Protection Laws* Clinton River Watershed Council, Utica, MI 1981

Environmental Defense Fund. *How Wet Is a Wetland? The Impacts of the Proposed Revisions to the Federal Wetlands Delineation Manual* Environmental Defense Fund and the World Wildlife Fund. Washington, D.C. 1992

Federal Interagency Committee for Wetland Delineation. *Federal Manual for Identifying and Delineating Jurisdictional Wetlands* A cooperative technical publication by U.S. Army Corps of Engineers, U.S. Environmental Protection Agency, U.S. Fish and Wildlife Service, and U.S.D.A. Soil Conservation Service, Washington, D.C. 1989

Fuller, Douglas. *Understanding, Living With, and Controlling Shoreline Erosion* Tip of the Mitt Watershed Council, Conway, MI 1995

Gruenwald, Gail S. *Michigan Wetlands: Yours to Protect* Tip of the Mitt Watershed Council, Conway, MI 1987

Hammer, Donald. *Creating Freshwater Wetlands* Lewis Publishers, Chelsea, MI 1992

Henderson, Carrol L. *Landscaping for Wildlife* Minnesota Department of Natural Resources, St. Paul, MN 1981

Kusler, J.A. *Our National Wetland Heritage: A Protection Guidebook* Environmental Law Institute, Washington, D.C. 1983

Kusler, J.A. and Mary E. Kentula. *Wetland Creation and Restoration: The Status of the Science* Island Press, Washington, D.C. 1990

Leopold, Aldo. *A Sand County Almanac* Oxford University Press, Inc., 1949

Marble, A.D. *A Guide to Wetland Functional Design* Lewis Publishers, Chelsea, MI 1992

Maryland Department of Natural Resources. *The Private Landowner's Wetlands Assistance Guide: Voluntary Options for Wetlands Stewardship in Maryland* Developed for workshops held in Eastern and Western Maryland, 1992

Michaud, Joy P. *At Home With Wetlands: A Landowner's Guide* Washington State Department of Ecology, Olympia, WA 1990

Michigan Department of Natural Resources. *A Wetland Conservation Strategy for Michigan* MDNR, Land and Water Management Division, Lansing, MI 1993

Michigan Department of Natural Resources. *Wetland Determination Manual Draft for Field Testing, Volume 1* MDNR, Land and Water Management Division, Lansing, MI 1989

Michigan Society of Planning Officials. *Community Planning Handbook: Tools and Techniques for Guiding Community Change* Michigan Society of Planning Officials, Rochester, MI 1991

Mitchell, M.K., and W.B. Stapp. *Field Manual for Water Quality Monitoring (Eighth Edition)* Thomson-Shore, Inc., Dexter, MI 1994

Mitsch, William J. and James G. Gosselink. *Wetlands: Second Edition* Van Nostrand Reinhold Company, Inc., New York NY 1993

Reed Jr., Porter B. *National List of Plant Species that Occur in Wetlands* U.S. Fish and Wildlife Service, Washington, D.C. 1988

Roth, E.M., R.D. Olsen, P.L. Snow, and R.R. Sumner. *Oregon Freshwater Wetland Assessment Methodology* Edited by S.G. McCannell. Oregon Division of State Lands, Salem, OR 1993

Scodari, Paul F. *Wetlands Protection: The Role of Economics* Environmental Law Institute, Washington, D.C. 1990

Smith, Helen V. *Michigan Wildflowers* Cranbrook Institute of Science, Bloomfield Hills, MI 1966

Small, Stephen J. *Preserving Family Lands: Essential Tax Strategies for the Landowner* Landowner Planning Center, Boston, MI 1992

Stone, W.A. and A.J.L. Stone. *Wetlands and Ground Water in the United States* American Groundwater Trust, Dublin, OH 1994

The Natural Lands Trust, Inc. *A Handbook for the Landowner: The Use and Protection of Privately Held Natural Lands* The Natural Lands Trust, Inc., Philadelphia, PA 1982

Thunhorst, G.A. *Wetland Planting Guide for the Northeastern United States* Environmental Concern, Inc., St Michaels, MD 1993

Tiner, Ralph "How Wet is a Wetland?" In V.2 N.3 *Great Lakes Wetlands* edited by Wilfred Cwikiel. Tip of the Mitt Watershed Council, Conway, MI 1991

Twolan-Strutt, Lisa. *Wetlands and Woodlots* Issues Paper, No. 1995-1. North American Wetlands Conservation Council (Canada), Ottawa, ONT 1995

U.S.D.A. Natural Resources Conservation Service. *Better Wetlands: More than a dozen ideas to improve restored wetlands for wildlife and personal enjoyment* USDA, Washington, D.C. 1995

U.S.D.A. Soil Conservation Service *Ponds: Planning, Design, and Construction* Agriculture Handbook 590, Washington D.C. 1971

U.S.D.A. Soil Conservation Service *Engineering Field Handbook, Chapter 13: Wetland Restoration, Enhancement, or Creation* Washington, D.C. 1992

U.S. Environmental Protection Agency, Region I. *The Federal Wetlands Protection Program in New England: A Guide to Section 404 for Citizens and States* U.S.E.P.A., Boston, MA 1991

U.S. Environmental Protection Agency, Office of Wetlands, Oceans, and Watersheds. *Natural Wetlands and Urban Stormwater: Potential Impacts and Management* U.S.E.P.A. Washington, D.C. 1991

Voss, Edward. *Michigan Flora Part I: Gymnosperms and Monocots* Cranbrook Institute of Science and University of Michigan Herbarium, Bloomfield Hills and Ann Arbor, MI 1972

Voss, Edward. *Michigan Flora Part 2: Dicots* Cranbrook Institute of Science and University of Michigan Herbarium, Bloomfield Hills and Ann Arbor, MI 1985